大学英语拓展课程系列教材

新编体育英语

NEW SPORTS ENGLISH 2

总主编 杨小彬　主编 常　娟
副主编 卢　洁　侯　润　杨　慧
编　者 杨　柳　熊召永　樊国刚　桂　滢　雷翠芳
　　　　黄　薇　董又能　夏少芳　王　瑰　张　路

清华大学出版社
北京

版权所有，侵权必究。举报：010-62782989，beiqinquan@tup.tsinghua.edu.cn。

图书在版编目（CIP）数据

新编体育英语. 2 / 常娟主编. —北京：清华大学出版社，2018（2024.9重印）
（大学英语拓展课程系列教材 / 杨小彬总主编）
ISBN 978-7-302-49691-5

Ⅰ. ①新… Ⅱ. ①常… Ⅲ. ①体育–英语–高等学校–教材 Ⅳ. ①G8

中国版本图书馆CIP数据核字（2018）第035214号

责任编辑：曹诗悦
封面设计：平　原
责任校对：王凤芝
责任印制：刘　菲

出版发行：清华大学出版社
　　　　网　　　址：https://www.tup.com.cn，https://www.wqxuetang.com
　　　　地　　　址：北京清华大学学研大厦A座　　邮　编：100084
　　　　社 总 机：010-83470000　　邮　购：010-62786544
　　　　投稿与读者服务：010-62776969，c-service@tup.tsinghua.edu.cn
　　　　质量反馈：010-62772015，zhiliang@tup.tsinghua.edu.cn
印 装 者：天津鑫丰华印务有限公司
经　　销：全国新华书店
开　　本：185mm×260mm　　印　张：9.25　　字　数：210千字
版　　次：2018年3月第1版　　　　　　　　印　次：2024年9月第5次印刷
定　　价：45.00元

产品编号：079068-02

⌘ 教材理念

　　高等教育国际化对大学英语教学提出了新的挑战和要求。2015年颁布的《国务院关于印发统筹推进世界一流大学和一流学科建设总体方案的通知》（国发〔2015〕64号）要求，高校应"加强创新创业教育，大力推进个性化培养，全面提升学生的综合素质、国际视野、科学精神和创业意识、创造能力"。《国家中长期教育改革和发展规划纲要（2010—2020年）》明确指出，高校要"适应国家经济社会对外开放要求，培养大批具有国际视野、通晓国际规则、能够参与国际事务和国际竞争的国际化人才"。在教育国际化的背景下，高等教育的使命之一就是为国家培养国际化人才，这其中，大学英语教学肩负着重要使命。

　　然而，国内部分高校对于大学英语教学的定位并不明确，盲目强调四六级英语证书的重要性，忽视学生专业发展的个性需求，从而导致学生英语学习积极性不高，课堂教学缺乏有效性。这在体育专业学生身上表现尤为突出。目前，随着体育文化交流与体育赛事日趋国际化，体育英语的重要性日益凸显。除了部分体育专业院校开设专业英语课程外，多数综合性大学的体育专业仍遵循传统的通用英语教学模式，缺乏渗透体育元素的专业英语熏陶。因此，我们有必要转变教学观念，在提高体育专业学生英语水平的基础上，融入一些体育英语知识，以提高体育专业学生大学英语课程学习的有效性和实用性。

　　本教材目标定位介于"通用英语"和"专门用途英语"之间，旨在帮助体育专业学生用英语获取专业领域知识，提高其语言应用能力，以适应未来职业发展的需要。具体来说，本教材希望提高学生的语言表达能力、语篇层次上的阅读能力、体育专业英语术语的理解和翻译能力，为他们将来从事体育教育、体育外事、体育新闻、体育研究等工作打下良好的基础。

⌘ 教材特色

　　本教材从主题内容、知识体系、活动练习等多方面精心策划，呈现以下特点：

1. 精心选材，内容新颖

　　本教材综合了体育学科下各专业特点，涉及体育项目、体育文化、传统体育以及运动体育科学等方面，视角多元，内容丰富。所选素材来源于国外网站最新的赛事规则、国际体育大会资料、技术手册以及国内外体育新闻报道和媒体评论等。教材编写时既考虑体育英语的原汁原味，又兼顾学生的语言实际水平，确保趣味性与实用性统一。

2. 科学编排，侧重实用

本教材针对体育相关专业学生的英语学习需求，加强语言技能训练，同时侧重对外体育交往中的实际应用，将日常生活与体育交往的不同场景交融在一起，真正培养学生的英语应用能力。

⌘ 教材框架

每单元的基本结构为：

第一部分：知识准备（Knowledge Preparation）。单元学习的准备部分，主要提供与本单元体育运动相关的概念、竞技规则或者文化背景知识等，帮助学生加深对单元主题体育运动的了解，完善其知识结构。

第二部分：阅读（Reading）。包括两篇主题课文，分别配有词汇和短语表以及相关练习。Text A 为精读课文，建议教师精讲精练；Text B 是对本单元话题的扩展或深化，目的在于开拓学生思路。练习活动丰富：课文理解题型包括文章框架图、细节多选题和对错判断等，注重引导学生在具体语境中学习专业知识，抓住关键信息，培养其归纳和演绎能力；词汇练习着重考查在语境中理解词义，练习所用语料均为原文原句，有相对完整的语境，注重原汁原味的语言表达；文中重难点句子的英汉互译练习，进一步提高学生的翻译能力。

第三部分：听说（Listening and Speaking）。根据单元主题设计两组任务。第一组为情景对话，第二组为短文理解。听说部分既有听前活动的热身，又有判断对错与多项选择等形式的理解练习，并配有词汇表。

第四部分：写作（Writing）。鼓励学生参照范例写作，写作文体涉及各类信函文书、个人简历、求职信等应用文体。

本教材内容安排灵活，教师可以根据授课计划、学生英语水平和专业特点，自主选取教学内容，因材施教，以培养学生英语应用能力、自主学习能力和体育文化素养。教材配有听力音频、电子课件、习题参考答案等教学资源，广大教师可下载参考*。

本教材编者团队为一线大学英语教师，均有教授体育专业学生大学英语课程的教学经历。教材编写分工如下：听力部分：王瑰（Units 1–4）、侯润（Units 5–8）；写作部分：常娟（Units 1–3, 6–8）、张路（Units 4–5）；阅读部分：熊召永（Unit 1）、樊国刚（Unit 2）、杨慧（Unit 3）、雷翠芳和桂滢（Unit 4）、夏少芳（Unit 5）、董又能和黄薇（Unit 6）、杨柳（Unit 7）、卢洁（Unit 8）。此外，本教材还有一支顾问团队，他们是具有国内外体育大赛裁判和体育教学经历且理论功底深厚的体育教师们，他们为教材的知识框架的建立提供了有力的专业保障。编写团队和顾问团队的合作确保了教材内容的准确性、语言的地道性和任务的真实性，保证了教材的质量。尽管如此，由于教材涉及大量体育专业知识，编者编写水平有限，书中不当之处在所难免，请各位专家和广大读者批评指正。

编者
2017 年 12 月于武汉

---

* 请登录 www.tsinghuaelt.com 下载。

Contents

Unit 1 Table Tennis
乒乓球 1

Text A Exploring ITTF......................... 3
Text B Ping-pong Diplomacy............ 10

Unit 2 Badminton
羽毛球 21

Text A Thomas Cup............................ 23
Text B Strategy for Badminton......... 30

Unit 3 Running and Jogging
跑步与慢跑 39

Text A Jogging...................................... 41
Text B Running for Weight Loss...... 46

Unit 4 Leisure Sports
休闲体育 53

Text A Chinese Golf   Chuiwan.... 54
Text B Sport Climbing Set to Be Olympic Sport for Tokyo 2020... 59

Unit 5 Dragon Dance and Lion Dance
舞龙和舞狮 67

Text A Dragon Dance......................... 69
Text B Lion Dance............................... 75

Unit 6 Sports Culture
体育文化 83

Text A Why Football Is Essential to American Culture.................... 84
Text B How the Internet Is Shaping Swim Culture........................... 90

Unit 7 Sports Science
体育科学 99

Text A Are Children Drinking Enough During Exercise?................... 101
Text B Training Healthy Youth Athletes.................................. 107

Unit 8 Skating
滑冰 115

Text A *Speed Skating*......................... 117
Text B *Ice Skating: Steps to Success*... 122

Part One — Knowledge Preparation

Table tennis or ping-pong, originated in Britain in 1890s, is an indoor sport in which two or four opponents use a small racket to hit a lightweight ball back and forth across a table divided by a net. Players must allow a ball played toward them to bounce one time on their side of the table, and must return it so that it bounces on the opposite side at least once. A point is scored when a player fails to return the ball within the rules. A game shall be won by the player first scoring 11 points unless both players score 10 points, when the game shall be won by the first player subsequently gaining a lead of 2 points.

Players demand quick reactions to hit the ball by driving, looping, pushing, blocking, chopping, etc. Matches are typically best of five or seven games. The event categories involve teams, singles, doubles and mixed doubles.

Table tennis is governed by the worldwide organization—International Table Tennis Federation (ITTF). It is now dubbed the National Ball Game in China.

乒乓球起源于19世纪90年代英国的一项室内运动，两名或四名对手在球网隔开的球桌上来回击球。球员须让来球在己方场地弹起一次才能还击过网，以落在对方台面上为有效，使对方不能接到来球或把球打回从而得分。一局比赛先得11分的球员获胜，若双方打成10平后，领先两分的球员获胜。

球员对来球需要迅速做出反应，击法主要有抽、拉、搓、挡、削等。比赛中一般采用五局三胜制或七局四胜制。比赛分团体、单打、双打、混双等数种。

乒乓球国际管理机构为国际乒乓球联合会（国际乒联）。乒乓球在中国被誉为"国球"。

Exploring ITTF

1. The International Table Tennis Federation (ITTF) is the governing body for all international table tennis associations. The role of the ITTF includes overseeing rules and regulations and seeking technological improvement for the sport of table tennis. The ITTF is responsible for the organization of numerous international competitions, including the World Table Tennis Championships.

2. The ITTF was founded in 1926, the founding members being Austria, Czechoslovakia, Denmark, England, Germany, Hungary, India, Sweden and Wales. The first international tournament was held in January 1926 in Berlin while the first World Table Tennis Championships was held in December 1926 in London.

3. The headquarters of the ITTF is in Lausanne, Switzerland. The previous president of the ITTF was Adham Sharara from Canada; the current president since 2014 is Thomas Weikert from Germany.

4. The ITTF recognizes six continental federations containing 226 members. Each continental federation has a president as its top official and owns its constitution. The following are recognized federations: ATTF (African Table Tennis Federation), ATTU (Asian Table Tennis Union), ETTU (European Table Tennis Union), ULTM (Latin American Table Tennis Union), NATTU (Northern American Table Tennis Union) and OTTF (Oceania Table Tennis Federation).

5. All member associations of the ITTF attend Annual General Meeting (AGM). Agendas on changes of the constitution, laws of table tennis, applications for membership, etc. are discussed and finalized through votes. Also, the president of ITTF, eight executive vice-presidents, and 32 or less continental representatives are elected at an AGM, serving for a four-year term. The president, executive vice-presidents, and the chairman of the athletes' commission compose the executive committee. The executive committee, continental representatives and presidents of the six continental federations or their appointees compose the board of directors (Board). The Board manages the work of the ITTF between AGMs. Several committees and commissions, working groups or panels work under the constitution of ITTF or under the Board.

6 Unlike the organizations for more popular sports, the ITTF tends to recognize teams from generally unrecognized governing bodies for disputed territory. For example, it currently recognizes the Table Tennis Federation of Kosovo even though Kosovo is excluded from most other sports. It recognized the People's Republic of China in 1953 and allowed some basic diplomacy which led to an opening for U.S. President Richard Nixon, called "Ping-pong Diplomacy", in the early 1970s.

7 Toward the end of 2000, the ITTF instituted several rules changes aimed at making table tennis more viable as a televised spectator sport. The older 38 mm balls were officially replaced by 40 mm balls. This increased the ball's air resistance and effectively slowed down the game.

8 The table tennis point system was reduced from a 21 to an 11-point scoring system in 2001. This was intended to make games more fast-paced and exciting. The ITTF also changed the rules on service to prevent a player from hiding the ball during service, in order to increase the average length of rallies and to reduce the server's advantage. Today, the game changes from time to time mainly to improve on the excitement for television viewers.

9 In 2007, ITTF's board of directors in Zagreb decided to implement the VOC-free glue rule at junior events, as a transitional period before the full implementation of the VOC ban on 1 September 2008. As of 1 January 2009, all speed glue was banned.

10 On 29 February 2008, the ITTF announced several rules changes after an ITTF Executive Meeting in Guangdong, China with regards to a player's eligibility to play for a new association. The new ruling is to encourage associations to develop their own players.

11 The ITTF is developing a "Table Tennis for ALL" program with the aim to make the sport popular, universal and inclusive. The term "ALL" means more people, but not only that, also different kinds of people in terms of age, gender, social status, culture and physical ability.

Word Bank

seek	[siːk]	v. 寻求；寻找
numerous	[ˈnuːmərəs]	adj. 许多的，很多的
found	[faʊnd]	v. 创立，建立，创办
previous	[ˈpriːviəs]	adj. 以前的，早先的
continental	[ˌkɑːntɪˈnentl]	adj. 大陆的；大洲的
constitution	[ˌkɑːnstəˈtuːʃn]	n. 章程；宪法；体制
union	[ˈjuːniən]	n. 联盟；协会
agenda	[əˈdʒendə]	n. 议程；日常工作事项；日程表
application	[ˌæplɪˈkeɪʃn]	n. 申请；应用
finalize	[ˈfaɪnəlaɪz]	v. 最后定下，使（计划、交易等）确定
commission	[kəˈmɪʃn]	n. 委员会；佣金
appointee	[əˌpɔɪnˈtiː]	n. 被任命者

panel	['pænl]	n. 咨询或研讨小组
disputed	[dɪ'spju:tid]	adj. 有争议的
territory	['terətɔ:ri]	n. 领土；领域；范围
opening	['oʊpnɪŋ]	n. 开始；机会；通路；空缺的职位
diplomacy	[dɪ'ploʊməsi]	n. 外交，外交手腕
institute	['ɪnstɪtu:t]	v. 开始（调查）；制定；创立
viable	['vaɪəbl]	adj. 可行的
spectator	['spekteɪtər]	n. 观众；旁观者
resistance	[rɪ'zɪstəns]	n. 阻力；抵抗，反抗；抵抗力
service	['sɜ:rvɪs]	n. 发球
rally	['ræli]	n.（网球、乒乓球等）连续对打；集会 v. 团结；集合
server	['sɜ:rvər]	n. 发球员
glue	[glu:]	n. 胶，胶水
transitional	[træn'zɪʃənl]	adj. 过渡的
ban	[bæn]	v. 禁止
eligibility	[ˌelɪdʒə'bɪləti]	n. 适任；合格；选举或参赛资格
universal	[ˌju:nɪ'vɜ:rsl]	adj. 普遍的，通用的；宇宙的，全世界的
inclusive	[ɪn'klu:sɪv]	adj. 包容的

Phrases

be excluded from	从……被排除
lead to	导致
be aimed at	目的是，旨在，针对
slow down	减速，放慢速度，使……慢下来
be intended to do something	意在做……，打算做……
as of	自……起
with regards to	关于
in terms of	依据，就……而言

Proper Names

International Table Tennis Federation (ITTF)	国际乒乓球联合会（国际乒联）
World Table Tennis Championships	世界乒乓球锦标赛
Czechoslovakia	（前）捷克斯洛伐克
Adham Sharara	阿德汉·沙拉拉（前任国际乒联主席）
Thomas Weikert	托马斯·维克特（现任国际乒联主席）
Table Tennis Federation of Kosovo	科索沃乒乓球协会

| Richard Nixon | 理查德·尼克松（美国前总统） |
| Zagreb | 萨格勒布（克罗地亚首都） |

Task 1 Text Organization

Read the text and fill in the blanks.

Paragraphs	Key Words	Supporting Details
Para. 1	The _____	• an international governing body for international _____ _____ associations • overseeing rules and regulations and seeking _____ improvement for the sport of table tennis • responsible for the organization of numerous international competitions including the _____
Paras. 2–10	Further introduction	• birth: (1) founded in _____ (2) headquartered in _____ • membership: (1) _____ members in 1926 (2) _____ continental confederations containing _____ members now • organizational structure: (1) AGM (2) the _____ committee (3) the _____ of directors • events and changes of rules: (1) It recognized the People's Republic of China in _____. (2) It changed the ball from 38 mm to _____ in 2000. (3) It reduced the point system from 21 to _____ point scoring system and changed the rules on service: serving without _____ the ball in 2001. (4) It implemented _____ in 2008. (5) It announced the rule changes about players' _____ to play for a new association in February 2008.

Unit 1
Table Tennis

| Para. 11 | "Table Tennis for All" program | • aim:
(1) to make the sport popular, _____ and _____.
(2) to bring the sport to more people and also different kinds of people in terms of age, gender, _____, culture and _____. |

Task 2 Reading Comprehension

Exercise 1

Read the text and decide whether the following statements are true (T) or false (F).

1. _____ The International Table Tennis Federation (ITTF) is the most important organization for all international table tennis associations.
2. _____ The six continental confederations are: Africa, Asia, Europe, Oceania, South America and North America.
3. _____ The first World Table Tennis Championships commenced in December 1926, in Berlin.
4. _____ The older 38 mm balls were replaced by 40 mm balls to increase the speed of ball.
5. _____ The ITTF allowed some basic diplomacy contributing to the U.S. President Richard Nixon's visit to China in the early 1970s, called "Ping-pong Diplomacy".

Exercise 2

Read the text and answer the following questions.

1. What does the ITTF stand for? What kind of organization is it?
2. What agendas are discussed and finalized at an AGM?
3. Who are elected at an AGM?
4. What is the executive committee composed of? What is the board of directors made up of?
5. Why did the ITTF reduce the point system from a 21 to an 11-point scoring system and change the rules on service?

Task 3 Language in Use

Exercise 1

Match the underlined words in the left column with their corresponding meanings in the right column.

1. The role of the ITTF includes overseeing rules and regulations and <u>seeking</u> technological improvement for the sport of table tennis.

2. The <u>previous</u> president of the ITTF was Adham Sharara from Canada.

3. Each continental federation has a president as its top official and owns its <u>constitution</u>.

4. <u>Agendas</u> on changes of the constitution, laws of table tennis, applications for membership, etc. are discussed and finalized through votes.

5. Several committees and commissions, working groups or <u>panels</u> work under the constitution of ITTF or under the Board.

6. For example, it currently recognizes the Table Tennis Federation of Kosovo even though Kosovo is <u>excluded</u> from most other sports.

7. It allowed some basic <u>diplomacy</u> which led to an opening for U.S. President Richard Nixon, called "Ping-pong Diplomacy", in the early 1970s.

8. Toward the end of 2000, the ITTF instituted several rules changes aimed at making table tennis more <u>viable</u> as a televised spectator sport.

9. The ITTF also changed the rules on service to prevent a player from hiding the ball during service, in order to increase the average length of <u>rallies</u> and to reduce the server's advantage.

A. a continuous series of shots that the players exchange without stopping as in playing table tennis, tennis, etc.

B. the job or activity of managing the relationships between countries

C. possible and likely to work well

D. not allowed to take part in something or to enter a place, especially in a way that seemed wrong or unfair

E. the qualification for being able to do something

F. a group of people with skills or specialist knowledge who have been chosen to give advice or opinions on a particular subject

G. a list of matters to be taken up (as at a meeting)

H. trying to find or gain

I. a set of basic laws and principles that a country or organization is governed by

10. On 29 February 2008, the ITTF announced several rules changes after an ITTF Executive Meeting in Guangdong, China with regards to a player's <u>eligibility</u> to play for a new association.

J. having happened or existed before

Exercise 2

Select one word or phrase for each blank from a list of choices given below and fill in the blank with its correct form.

| aim at | spectator | slow down | official | govern |
| oversee | agenda | current | tend | lead to |

The worldwide organization International Table Tennis Federation (ITTF) is the most important body that **1.**_____ the various competitions of table tennis all over the world, including the World Table Tennis Championships. Its main role involves **2.**_____ rules and regulations and seeking technological improvement for the sport of table tennis. Its member associations have developed from the original 9 to the **3.**_____ 226. All member associations must attend annual general meeting whose **4.**_____ are discussed and finalized through votes.

The ITTF **5.**_____ to recognize teams from the disputed territory. In 1953, it recognized China. Its flexible policy **6.**_____ the success of Chinese Ping-pong Diplomacy and U.S. President Richard Nixon's visit to Beijing in the early 1970s.

In 2000, the ITTF made some rule changes which were **7.**_____ making table tennis competitions more exciting for the television **8.**_____. 40 mm balls **9.**_____ took the place of the older 38 mm balls, which increased the ball's air resistance and effectively **10.**_____ the game.

Exercise 3

Translate the following sentences into English.

1. 关于球员的参赛资格俱乐部做了一些规定。(with regards to)
2. 就其特点而言，乒乓球运动适合每个人。(in terms of)
3. 由于受伤，他没被列入参赛名单。(be excluded from)
4. 为了使球速放缓，小球被改成了大球。(slow down)
5. 乒乓球规则的改变旨在让电视观众更好地观看比赛。(be aimed at doing something)

Text B

Ping-pong Diplomacy

Ping-pong diplomacy refers to the exchange of table tennis players between the United States and People's Republic of China (PRC) in the early 1970s. This event marked a thaw in Sino-American relations that paved the way for a visit to Beijing by President Richard Nixon.

Background

In the 1950s, the United States viewed the People's Republic of China as an aggressor nation and enforced an economic containment policy including an embargo. After approximately twenty years of neither diplomatic nor economic relations, both countries finally saw an advantage in opening up to each other. The thirty-first World Table Tennis Championships, held in Nagoya, Japan, provided an opportunity for both China and the United States.

Process

The U.S. table tennis team was in Nagoya, Japan in 1971 for the 31st World Table Tennis Championships on April 6 when they received an invitation to visit China. From the early years of the People's Republic of China, sports had played an important role in diplomacy, often incorporating the slogan "Friendship First, Competition Second". During the isolated years, athletes were among the few PRC nationals who were allowed to travel overseas. This World Table Tennis Championships marked the return of China's participation after a six-year absence. On April 10, 1971, the team and accompanying journalists became the first American delegation to set foot in the Chinese capital since 1949.

According to the *History of U.S. Table Tennis* by Tim Boggan, who went to China along with the U.S. table tennis team, the greatest incident that may have triggered the invitation from China perhaps was the unexpected but dramatic meeting between the flamboyant American player Glenn Cowan and the Chinese player Zhuang Zedong, a three-time world champion and winner of many other table tennis events. Zhuang Zedong described the incident in a 2007 talk at the USC U.S.-China Institute.

The events leading up to the encounter began when Glenn Cowan missed his team bus one afternoon after his practice in Nagoya during the 31st World Table Tennis Championships. Cowan had been practicing for 15 minutes with the Chinese player, Liang Geliang, when a Japanese official came and wanted to close the training area. As Cowan looked in vain for his team bus, a Chinese player waved to him to get on his Chinese team bus. Moments after his casual talking through an interpreter to the Chinese players, Zhuang Zedong came up from his back seat to greet him and presented him with a silk-screen portrait of Huangshan Mountains, a famous product from Hangzhou. Cowan wanted to give something back, but all he could find from his bag was a comb.

The American hesitantly replied, "I can't give you a comb. I wish I could give you something, but I can't." On the following day, many Japanese newspapers carried photographs of Zhuang Zedong and Glenn Cowan. Glenn Cowan later bought a T-shirt with a red, white and blue, peace emblem flag and the words "Let It Be", which he presented to Zhuang Zedong at another chance meeting.

Results and Legacy

Ping-pong diplomacy was successful and resulted in opening the U.S.-PRC relationship, leading the U.S. to lift the embargo against China on June 10, 1971.

Two months after Richard Nixon's visit, Zhuang Zedong visited the U.S. as the head of a Chinese table tennis delegation, April 12–30, 1972.

In 1988, table tennis became an Olympic sport.

During the week of June 9, 2008, a three-day Ping-pong Diplomacy event was held at the Richard Nixon Presidential Library and Museum in California. Original members of both the Chinese and American ping-pong teams from 1971 were present and competed again.

Ping-pong diplomacy was referenced in the 1994 film *Forrest Gump*. After suffering injuries in battle, Forrest develops an aptitude for the sport and joins the U.S. Army team—eventually competing against Chinese teams on a goodwill tour.

Word Bank

Word	Pronunciation	Meaning
exchange	[ɪksˈtʃeɪndʒ]	n. 交换；交流；交易所；兑换
thaw	[θɔː]	n. 解冻；融雪
aggressor	[əˈgresər]	n. 侵略者，侵略国；挑衅者
enforce	[ɪnˈfɔːrs]	v. 实施，执行
containment	[kənˈteɪnmənt]	n. 牵制（遏制）政策
embargo	[ɪmˈbɑːrgoʊ]	n. 贸易禁令，禁运
approximately	[əˈprɑːksɪmətli]	adv. 大约，近似地，近于
diplomatic	[ˌdɪpləˈmætɪk]	adj. 外交的，外交上的；老练的
incorporate	[ɪnˈkɔːrpəreɪt]	v. 包含；结合
slogan	[ˈsloʊgən]	n. 口号；标语
isolated	[ˈaɪsəleɪtɪd]	adj. 孤立的，隔离的
national	[ˈnæʃnəl]	n. 国民
participation	[pɑːrˌtɪsɪˈpeɪʃn]	n. 参与
accompany	[əˈkʌmpəni]	v. 陪伴，伴随；伴奏
delegation	[ˌdelɪˈgeɪʃn]	n. 代表团
trigger	[ˈtrɪgər]	v. 引发，引起，触发
flamboyant	[flæmˈbɔɪənt]	adj. 炫耀的；火焰似的；艳丽的
encounter	[ɪnˈkaʊntər]	n. 遭遇；偶然碰见

wave	[weɪv]	v.	挥手示意；使成波浪形
casual	[ˈkæʒuəl]	adj.	随便的；非正式的
interpreter	[ɪnˈtɜːrprɪtər]	n.	解释者；口译者，翻译
hesitantly	[ˈhezɪtəntli]	adv.	迟疑地，踌躇地
comb	[koʊm]	n.	梳子
emblem	[ˈembləm]	n.	标志；徽章，纹章
legacy	[ˈleɡəsi]	n.	遗赠；遗产
original	[əˈrɪdʒɪnl]	adj.	原始的，最初的；独创的，新颖的
reference	[ˈrefrəns]	v.	引用
aptitude	[ˈæptɪtuːd]	n.	天资，天赋
eventually	[ɪˈventʃuəli]	adv.	最后，终于
goodwill	[ˌɡʊdˈwɪl]	n.	好意，亲善，友善

Phrases

open up to	对……开放
pave the way for	为……做好准备；为……铺平道路
provide… for…	为……提供……
play an important role in	在……起重要作用
set foot in	踏进，踏入，涉足
present… with/to …	把……赠送给……
in vain	徒劳地，无益地，白白地
result in	导致，引起，结果是

Proper Names

Nagoya	名古屋（日本本州岛中南岸港市）
Tim Boggan	蒂姆·博甘（前美国乒乓球队队员）
Glenn Cowan	格伦·考恩（前美国乒乓球队队员）
Zhuang Zedong	庄则栋（前中国乒乓球队队员、世界冠军）
USC U.S.-China Institute	南加州大学美中研究所
Liang Geliang	梁戈亮（前中国乒乓球队队员、世界冠军）
Richard Nixon Presidential Library and Museum	尼克松总统图书馆暨博物馆
Forrest Gump	《阿甘正传》（电影名）

Critical Reading and Thinking

Read the text and decide whether the following statements are true (T) or false (F).

1. _____ Ping-pong diplomacy refers to the exchange of table tennis players between the United States and People's Republic of China (PRC) in the early 1960s.
2. _____ Shortly after the founding of the People's Republic of China, the United States took a friendly policy toward China.
3. _____ The thirty-second World Table Tennis Championships was held in Nagoya, Japan.
4. _____ During the isolated years, athletes were among the few PRC nationals who were allowed to go abroad.
5. _____ The Chinese table tennis team had been absent in the World Table Tennis Championships for six years by 1971.
6. _____ According to the *History of U.S. Table Tennis*, the greatest incident that may have led to the invitation from China perhaps was the unexpected but dramatic meeting between the American player Tim Boggan and the Chinese player Zhuang Zedong.
7. _____ During the chance meeting Zhuang Zedong sent the American player a silk-screen portrait of Huangshan Mountains as a gift.
8. _____ The success of Ping-pong Diplomacy led to the opening of Sino-American relations and the ending of the U.S. embargo against China.
9. _____ Since 1988, table tennis has been an Olympic sport.
10. _____ From June 9, 2008, a three-day Ping-pong Diplomacy event was held in California between the original Chinese ping-pong team and the original American ping-pong team from 1971.

Translation

Translate the following sentences into Chinese.

1. This event marked a thaw in Sino-American relations that paved the way for a visit to Beijing by President Richard Nixon.
2. After approximately twenty years of neither diplomatic nor economic relations, both countries finally saw an advantage in opening up to each other.
3. From the early years of the People's Republic of China, sports had played an important role in diplomacy, often incorporating the slogan "Friendship First, Competition Second".
4. On April 10, 1971, the team and accompanying journalists became the first American delegation to set foot in the Chinese capital since 1949.
5. After suffering injuries in battle, Forrest develops an aptitude for the sport and joins the U.S. Army team—eventually competing against Chinese teams on a goodwill tour.

Part Three — Listening and Speaking

Task 1

Word Bank

gold medal		金牌
excel	[ɪk'sel]	v. 擅长；超过
track and field		田径；田径赛
keen on		喜爱，热衷于……
swing	[swɪŋ]	v. 挥舞；摇摆，摆动
racket	['rækɪt]	n. 球拍
bounce	[baʊns]	v. 弹跳，使弹起
spin	[spɪn]	n. 旋转
strategy	['strætədʒi]	n. 策略
serve	[sɜːrv]	v. 发球
tactic	['tæktɪk]	n. 策略

Listen to a radio program and answer the following questions.

1. What is this radio program about?
2. What is the Chinese national sport?
3. According to the radio program, what sport are Americans good at?
4. Why do Chinese people often win the table tennis competitions?

Task 2

Word Bank

Grand Slam		大满贯
eye-catching		adj. 引人注目的，显著的
semifinal	[ˌsemi'faɪnl]	n. 半决赛
matchup	['mætʃʌp]	n. 比赛；匹配
Belarus		白俄罗斯
ITTF World Tour China Open		国际乒联世界巡回赛中国公开赛
adjustment	[ə'dʒʌstmənt]	n. 调整

Unit 1
Table Tennis

jet lag		时差
titleholder	['taɪtl hoʊldər]	n. 冠军保持者
enthusiastic	[ɪnˌθuːziˈæstɪk]	adj. 热情的；热心的；热烈的，狂热的
quarterfinal	[ˌkwɔːrtər ˈfaɪnl]	n. 四分之一决赛

Listen to a news report about table tennis and fill in the blanks with the information you hear.

"He has shown much **1.**_____. We once played in the same **2.**_____, so he was quite **3.**_____ with my style. Playing three matches today, I was **4.**_____ affected, especially being **5.**_____ into the decisive game after leading 3-1 due to lack of **6.**_____," said Zhang.

"Hoping that both of us can put on a show for these **7.**_____ crowds," Ma talked about Sunday's **8.**_____ between the two Olympic singles gold medalists.

Xu Xin failed to secure the men's singles **9.**_____ for the Chinese team after losing to Wong Chunting of Hong Kong, China 4-3. Wong will meet world No. 2 Fan Zhendong, who beat Zhou Yu 4-2 in an all-Chinese **10.**_____.

Task 3

Listen to the five sentences from the recording, repeat each sentence after it is spoken, and then write it down.

1. _____.
2. _____.
3. _____.
4. _____.
5. _____.

Task 4

Discuss the following questions in your group.

1. Can you talk about one table tennis player that you know?
2. Why is Chinese table tennis team so competitive?

Letter Format

Although people write different kinds of letters for different purposes, a formal letter usually includes the following elements: heading, date, inside address, salutation, body, complimentary closing and signature, as illustrated below.

Heading (Sender's address)

Date (Month, Day, Year)

Inside Address (Recipient's name, title and address)

Salutation (Name of recipient),

Body Paragraph 1

Body Paragraph 2

Body Paragraph 3

Complimentary Close (Sincerely...),

Signature

P.S.

On the left corner below the signature, if you want to add any additional information to the letter, you write a "P.S." (post script) and the message after that; if you want to attach a document, you write "Enclosure /Encl./ Enc.". For example, "Encl. Résumé" indicates that a résumé is enclosed with this letter, and "Enclosure (2)" means there are two documents attached to the letter.

However, letters do not always contain all the elements. The elements above are for formal letters, for those friendly letters, inside address can be omitted.

There are also several types of letter format. Compare the following letters, can you identify the differences among them? Sample 1 applies block style, Sample 2 modified block style, and Sample 3 indented style. Although all of them can be used in letter writing, block style is more preferable and indented style is considered traditional or even out of date now.

Sample 1   A letter in block style

School of Sport Education

Hubei University

368 Youyi Avenue

Wu Han

Hubei Province

430062

April 7, 2010

Li Xingguang

Personnel Manager

Little Sport Star International Training Center

322# Luoyu Road

Wuhan

Hubei Province

430076

Dear Mr. Li,

In reply to your advertisement in *Chutian Metropolitan* of April 6, I respectfully offer my services for the position of table tennis trainer.

I am twenty years old and going to graduate from Hubei University. I am a Sport Education major. Besides, I've learned English for more than eight years and I am excellent in table tennis. In the last three years, I've been one of the trainers of our campus table tennis club, which makes me experienced in training work. I do well in my study and my scores are outstanding in my class. From above-mention, I am sure that I will be qualified for the position.

I welcome the opportunity to meet with you to further discuss my qualifications and your needs. Thank you for your time and consideration.

Sincerely yours,

Zhang Hong

Zhang Hong

Sample 2 A letter in modified block style

School of Sport Education
Hubei University
368 Youyi Avenue
Wu Han
Hubei Province
430062

April 7, 2010

Li Xingguang
Personnel Manager
Little Sport Star International Training Center
322# Luoyu Road
Wuhan
Hubei Province
430076

Dear Mr. Li,

In reply to your advertisement in *Chutian Metropolitan* of April 6, I respectfully offer my services for the position of table tennis trainer.

I am twenty years old and going to graduate from Hubei University. I am a Sport Education major. Besides, I've learned English for more than eight years and I am excellent in table tennis. In the last three years, I've been one of the trainers of our campus table tennis club, which makes me experienced in training work. I do well in my study and my scores are outstanding in my class. From above-mention, I am sure that I will be qualified for the position.

I welcome the opportunity to meet with you to further discuss my qualifications and your needs. Thank you for your time and consideration.

Sincerely yours,

Zhang Hong
Zhang Hong

Sample 3 A letter in indented style

School of Sport Education
Hubei University
368 Youyi Avenue
Wu Han
Hubei Province
430062

April 7, 2010

Li Xingguang
Personnel Manager
Little Sport Star International Training Center
322# Luoyu Road
Wuhan
Hubei Province
430076

Dear Mr. Li,

  In reply to your advertisement in *Chutian Metropolitan* of April 6, I respectfully offer my services for the position of table tennis trainer.

  I am twenty years old and going to graduate from Hubei University. I am a Sport Education major. Besides, I've learned English for more than eight years and I am excellent in table tennis. In the last three years, I've been one of the trainers of our campus table tennis club, which makes me experienced in training work. I do well in my study and my scores are outstanding in my class. From above-mention, I am sure that I will be qualified for the position.

  I welcome the opportunity to meet with you to further discuss my qualifications and your needs. Thank you for your time and consideration.

Sincerely yours,

Zhang Hong
Zhang Hong

Follow-up Writing

Put the following sections together and form a complete letter.

A

We look forward to seeing you there!

B

Susan Harris

C

My name is Susan Harris and I am writing on behalf of the organizing committee of the Table Tennis Festival hosted by Lockwood Middle School.

D

Dear Mrs. Collins:

E

December 10, 2008

F

A significant amount of the students at local middle schools have joined in the Table Tennis Festival which provides them with chances to practice table tennis and organizes matches among different schools. As the festival is approaching, you are invited to attend the final and give an address to the closing ceremony.

G

Mrs. Jody Collins
President
Lockwood Table Tennis Association
23 Main Street
Lockwood, NJ

H

Sincerely,

I

As one of the prominent figures in the field, you are earnestly expected by all of us, and we would be honored by your attendance. Our final and closing ceremony will be held at our school stadium on January 16th. Please reply by Monday the 9th of January to confirm your attendance.

J

Lockwood Middle School
307 Main Street
Lockwood, NJ 51686

K

Susan Harris

Part One — Knowledge Preparation

Badminton is a racquet sport played using racquets to hit a shuttlecock across a net. Although it may be played with larger teams, the most common forms of the game are "singles" (with one player per side) and "doubles" (with two players per side). Badminton is often played as a casual outdoor activity in a yard or on a beach; formal games are played on a rectangular indoor court. Points are scored by striking the shuttlecock with the racquet and landing it within the opposing side's half of the court.

The game developed in British India from the earlier game of battledore and shuttlecock. European play came to be dominated by Denmark but the game has become very popular in Asia, with recent competitions dominated by China. Since 1992, badminton has been a Summer Olympic sport with five events: men's singles, women's singles, men's doubles, women's doubles, and mixed doubles. At high levels of play, the sport demands excellent fitness: players require aerobic stamina, agility, strength, speed, and precision. It is also a technical sport, requiring good motor coordination and the development of sophisticated racquet movements.

羽毛球运动是一项隔着球网、用球拍击打羽毛球的运动项目。虽然也可以进行团体比赛，但最常见的比赛形式还是"单打"（一边一人）和"双打"（一边两人）。人们也常常把它作为一项可以在庭院或海滩进行的户外休闲活动；而正规的羽毛球比赛是在长方形的室内场地举行的。用球拍击打羽毛球使之落在对方一边场地内即可得分。

这项运动起源于早期英属印度的一项板羽球游戏。丹麦羽毛球队曾在欧洲一枝独秀，但近年来这项运动风靡亚洲，从最近的战绩来看，中国队独领风骚。羽毛球运动于1992年进入夏季奥运会，共设五个项目：男子单打、女子单打、男子双打、女子双打以及男女混合双打。高水平的羽毛球比赛需要超强的身体素质：运动员需要具备超强的有氧耐力、灵活性、力量、速度与精准度。此外，羽毛球也是一项技巧运动，需要球员具备良好的运动协调性并掌握复杂的球拍使用技巧。

Part Two   Reading

Text A

Thomas Cup

1 The Thomas Cup, sometimes called the World Men's Team Championships, is an international badminton competition among teams representing member nations of the Badminton World Federation (BWF), the sport's global governing body. The championships have been conducted every two years since the 1982 tournament, amended from being conducted every three years since the first tournament held in 1948–1949.

2 The Thomas Cup competition was the idea of Sir George Alan Thomas, a highly successful English badminton player of the early 1900s, who was inspired by tennis's Davis Cup, and football's World Cup first held in 1930. His idea was well received at the general meeting of the International Badminton Federation (IBF, now Badminton World Federation) in 1939.

3 In the same year, Sir George presented the Thomas Cup, officially known as The International Badminton Championship Challenge Cup, produced by Atkin Bros. of London at a cost of $40,000. The Cup stands 28 inches high and 16 inches across at its widest, and consists of three parts: a plinth, a bowl, and a lid with player figure.

4 The first tournament was held in 1948–1949 when ten national teams participated in the first Thomas Cup competition. Three qualifying zones were established: Pan America, Europe, and the Pacific; though Malaya (now Malaysia) was the only Pacific zone participant. In a format that would last until 1984, all matches between nations would consist of nine individual matches; the victorious nation needing to win at least five of these contests. The United States and Denmark won their respective zone qualifications and thus joined Malaya for the inter-zone matches. In the final round held in Preston, England, Malaya beat Denmark 8-1 and became the first nation to win a Thomas Cup.

5 In the early 1980s the IBF (BWF) revamped the format of Thomas Cup. Starting in 1984 it was held every two years not three. Matches between nations at all stages of the Thomas Cup were trimmed from nine matches to five, played in one day not two. Lineups continued to consist of three singles players and two doubles teams, but each now played a single match against the opposing team's counterpart.

6　From 1984 through 2002 the final phase of Thomas Cup competition brought eight competing teams together. These included the defending champion nation and the host nation exempt from earlier qualification matches. The eight teams were divided into pools or groups of four. Round-robin play within each group determined first and second place group finishers who then advanced to the semifinals. Each semifinal match pitted the top finisher in one group against the second-place finisher in the other, with the winners proceeding to the championship match. A playoff for third place between losing semifinalists was instituted in 1984 but was dropped in 1990.

7　From 2014, 16 teams were presented in the tournament. Teams no longer qualifying via the continental championships, instead teams will be invited based on their World Ranking position. The new structure also ensured a minimum of one team from each continent and three teams from Asia and Europe will qualify. However, BWF reverted to old qualifying system in 2016 tournament.

8　Of the 28 Thomas Cup tournaments held since 1948–1949, only five nations have won the title. Indonesia is the most successful team, having won the tournament 13 times. China, which did not begin to compete until the 1982 series, follows Indonesia with nine titles, including five consecutive titles in 2004, 2006, 2008, 2010 and 2012. Malaysia has won five titles. Japan and Denmark both have one. Thomas Cup is possibly the world's "biggest" and most prestigious regularly-held badminton events in terms of player and fan interest. For many they trump major tournaments for individual competitors such as the venerable All-England Championships, the BWF World Championships, and even the badminton competitions at the Olympic Games.

Word Bank

conduct	[kən'dʌkt]	v. 组织并实施
tournament	['tʊrnəmənt]	n. 锦标赛，联赛；比赛
amend	[ə'mend]	v. 修改；改善，改进
inspire	[ɪn'spaɪər]	v. 激发；鼓舞；启示，使生灵感
present	[prɪ'zent]	v. 提出；介绍；呈现；赠送
officially	[ə'fɪʃəli]	adv. 正式地；官方地
plinth	[plɪnθ]	n. 柱基，底座
lid	[lɪd]	n. 盖子；眼睑
qualify	['kwɑːlɪfaɪ]	v. 取得资格，有资格
establish	[ɪ'stæblɪʃ]	v. 建立，创办；安置
participant	[pɑːr'tɪsɪpənt]	n. 参与者
format	['fɔːrmæt]	n. 格式；版式；赛制
victorious	[vɪk'tɔːriəs]	adj. 胜利的，凯旋的
respective	[rɪ'spektɪv]	adj. 分别的，各自的
inter-zone	[ɪntə'zoʊn]	adj. 地区间的；地带间的

revamp	['riːvæmp]	v. 修改；修补；翻新
trim	[trɪm]	v. 削减；修剪；整理；装点
opposing	[ə'pəʊzɪŋ]	adj. 反对的；相对的；对面的
phase	[feɪz]	n. 时期
pool	[puːl]	n. 小组；撞球；水塘；共同资金
round-robin	[ˌraʊnd'rɑːbɪn]	n. 循环赛；[计] 循环
determine	[dɪ'tɜːmɪn]	v. 决定；判定，判决；限定
finisher	['fɪnɪʃər]	n. 整理工；修整器；决定性的事件；最后优胜者
semifinalist	[ˌsemi'faɪnəlɪst]	n. 成功晋级半决赛的选手，半决赛选手
via	['vaɪə]	prep. 通过；经由
ensure	[ɪn'ʃʊr]	v. 保证，确保；使安全
continent	['kɑːntɪnənt]	n. 大陆，洲；陆地
consecutive	[kən'sekjətɪv]	adj. 连贯的，连续不断的
prestigious	[pre'stɪdʒəs]	adj. 有名望的，享有声望的
trump	[trʌmp]	v. 胜过；打出王牌赢
venerable	['venərəbl]	adj. 庄严的；值得尊敬的；珍贵的

Phrases

at its widest	最宽
consist of	包含，由……组成；充斥着
proceed to	继续下去；进入……
advance to	达到 (某地等)；前进到
pit against	使竞争，与……对阵
be presented in	出席，在席
exempt from	豁免，免除
a minimum of	至少，最少
revert to	回复；回归
in terms of	依据，按照；在……方面

Proper Names

Thomas Cup	汤姆斯杯
Badminton World Federation (BWF)	羽毛球世界联合会
Sir George Alan Thomas	乔治·艾伦·汤姆斯爵士
Davis Cup	戴维斯杯（国际网球赛）

World Cup	世界杯足球赛
International Badminton Federation	国际羽毛球联合会（后更名为羽毛球世界联合会）
The International Badminton Championship Challenge Cup	国际羽毛球锦标赛挑战杯
Atkin Bros.	阿特金兄弟公司
Pan America	泛美洲地区
Malaya	马来亚；马来半岛
Pacific	太平洋
Denmark	丹麦（欧洲国家）
World Ranking	世界排名
Indonesia	印度尼西亚（东南亚岛国）
All-England Championships	全英羽毛球锦标赛
BWF World Championships	世界羽毛球锦标赛

Task 1 Text Organization

Read the text and fill in the blanks.

Paragraphs	Key Words	Supporting Details
Para. 1	A brief introduction to the Thomas Cup	• The Thomas Cup, also _____ the World Men's Team Championships, is an _____ badminton competition among teams representing member nations of the Badminton World Federation (BWF), the sport's _____ governing body. • The championships have been conducted every _____ years since the 1982 tournament, amended from being conducted every _____ years since the first tournament held in 1948–1949.

26

Unit 2
Badminton

Paras. 2–7	History and development of the Thomas Cup	• The Thomas Cup competition was the _____ of Sir George Alan Thomas, and was well _____ at the general meeting of the International Badminton Federation (IBF, now BWF) in 1939. • The Cup stands _____ inches high and _____ inches across at its widest, and consists of _____ parts: a plinth, a bowl, and a lid with _____ figure. • In the first Thomas Cup competition, _____ beat Denmark 8–1 and became the first nation to win a Thomas Cup. • In the early 1980s the IBF (BWF) _____ the format of Thomas Cup. • From 1984 through 2002 the final phase of Thomas Cup competition brought _____ competing teams together. These included the _____ champion nation and the _____ nation exempt from earlier qualification matches. • From 2014, _____ teams were presented in the tournament. Teams no longer _____ via the continental championships, instead teams will be _____ based on their World Ranking position.
Para. 8	Results of the Thomas Cup	• Of the 28 Thomas Cup tournaments held since 1948–1949, only _____ nations have won the title. • _____ is the most successful team, having won the tournament 13 times. • China, which did not begin to compete until the 1982 series, follows Indonesia with _____ titles, including _____ consecutive titles in 2004, 2006, 2008, 2010 and 2012.

Task 2 Reading Comprehension

Exercise 1

Read the text and decide whether the following statements are true (T) or false (F).

1. _____ The Thomas Cup was named after Sir George Alan Thomas, a highly successful English badminton player of the early 1900s.

2. _____ The Thomas Cup was held every four years in different countries in the world.

3. _____ The Thomas Cup, officially known as The International Badminton Championship Challenge Cup, was donated by Sir George Alan Thomas.

4. _____ To take part in the final phase of Thomas Cup competition, teams still have to qualify via the continental championships now.

5. _____ All the titles of Thomas Cup are won by Asian national teams except for one won by Denmark.

Exercise 2

Read the text and answer the following questions.

1. When and where was the first Thomas Cup competition held?
2. How does the Thomas Cup look like?
3. What do you know about the lineups of teams in the Thomas Cup?
4. How many teams can participate in the final phase of Thomas Cup now?
5. How many teams have won the title of Thomas Cup, and how many times each team won respectively?

Task 3 Language in Use

Exercise 1

Match the underlined words or phrases in the left column with their corresponding meanings in the right column.

1. The championships have been <u>conducted</u> every two years since the 1982 tournament.

   A. formal; approved by the government or by someone in authority

2. His idea was well <u>received</u> at the general meeting of the International Badminton Federation in 1939.

   B. created; set up

3. The Thomas Cup was <u>officially</u> known as The International Badminton Championship Challenge Cup.

   C. organized and done

4. In the early 1980s the IBF <u>revamped</u> the format of Thomas Cup.

   D. having reputation; respected

5. Three qualifying zones were <u>established</u>: Pan America, Europe, and the Pacific.

   E. to excuse from a duty

6. Matches between nations at all stages of the Thomas Cup were <u>trimmed</u> from nine matches to five.

F. welcomed; accepted

7. These included the defending champion nation and the host nation <u>exempt from</u> earlier qualification matches.

G. went back to

8. However, BWF <u>reverted to</u> old qualifying system in 2016 tournament.

H. impressive because it is old or important historically

9. Thomas Cup is possibly the world's "biggest" and most <u>prestigious</u> regularly held badminton events in terms of player and fan interest.

I. made changes in order to improve it

10. For many they trump major tournaments for individual competitors such as the <u>venerable</u> All-England Championships.

J. reduced slightly in extent or size

 Exercise 2

Select one word for each blank from a list of choices given below and fill in the blank with its correct form.

| revamp | consecutive | trim | prestigious | amend |
| revert | inspire | receive | conduct | present |

The Thomas Cup is an international badminton competition. The championships have been **1.**_____ every two years since the 1982 tournament, **2.**_____ from being conducted every three years since the first tournament held in 1948–1949. It was the idea of Sir George Alan Thomas, who was **3.**_____ by tennis's Davis Cup, and football's World Cup. This idea was well **4.**_____ at the general meeting of the International Badminton Federation in 1939. Sir George **5.**_____ the Thomas Cup, which is 28 inches high and 16 inches across at its widest, and consists of three parts: a plinth, a bowl, and a lid with player figure.

The first tournament was held in 1948–1949 when ten national teams participated in it. In the final round, Malaya beat Denmark and became the first nation to win a Thomas Cup. In the early 1980s the IBF (now BWF) **6.**_____ the format of Thomas Cup. Starting in 1984 it was held every two years not three. Matches between nations at all stages of the Thomas Cup were **7.**_____ from nine matches to five, played in one day not two. From 1984 through 2002 the final phase of Thomas Cup competition brought eight competing teams together. From 2014, 16 teams were presented in the tournament. Teams no longer qualifying via the continental championships, instead teams will be invited based on their World Ranking position. However,

BWF **8.**_____ to old qualifying system in 2016 tournament.

Of the 28 Thomas Cup tournaments, only five nations have won the title. Indonesia is the most successful team, having won the tournament 13 times. China follows Indonesia with nine titles, including five **9.**_____ titles. Malaysia has won five titles. Japan and Denmark both have one. Thomas Cup is possibly the world's "biggest" and most **10.**_____ regularly-held badminton events in terms of player and fan interest.

 Exercise 3

Translate the following sentences into English.
1. 他的话激发了我的自信心。(inspire)
2. 他不能胜任自己的场上位置。(be qualified for)
3. 椅子是由椅座和椅背构成的。(consist of)
4. 由于年龄太小，他被免除刑事责任。(exempt from)
5. 中国仅次于印度尼西亚赢得九次桂冠，其中包括一次五连冠。(follow; consecutive)

Text B

Strategy for Badminton

To win in badminton, players need to employ a wide variety of strokes in the right situations. These range from powerful jumping smashes to delicate tumbling net returns. Often rallies finish with a smash, but setting up the smash requires subtler strokes. For example, a netshot can force the opponent to lift the shuttlecock, which gives an opportunity to smash. If the netshot is tight and tumbling, then the opponent's lift will not reach the back of the court, which makes the subsequent smash much harder to return.

Deception is also important. Expert players prepare for many different strokes that look identical, and use slicing to deceive their opponents about the speed or direction of the stroke. If an opponent tries to anticipate the stroke, he may move in the wrong direction and may be unable to change his body momentum in time to reach the shuttlecock.

Singles

Since one person needs to cover the entire court, singles tactics are based on forcing the opponent to move as much as possible; this means that singles strokes are normally directed to the corners of the court. Players exploit the length of the court by combining lifts and clears with drop shots and net shots. Smashing tends to be less prominent in singles than in doubles because the smasher has no partner to follow up his effort and is thus vulnerable to a skillfully placed return.

Moreover, frequent smashing can be exhausting in singles where the conservation of a player's energy is at a premium. However, players with strong smashes will sometimes use the shot to create openings, and players commonly smash weak returns to try to end rallies.

In singles, players will often start the rally with a forehand high serve or with a flick serve. Low serves are also used frequently, either forehand or backhand. Drive serves are rare.

At high levels of play, singles demands extraordinary fitness. Singles is a game of patient positional manoeuvring, unlike the all-out aggression of doubles.

Doubles

Both pairs will try to gain and maintain the attack, smashing downwards when the opportunity arises. Whenever possible, a pair will adopt an ideal attacking formation with one player hitting down from the rearcourt, and his partner in the midcourt intercepting all smash returns except the lift. If the rearcourt attacker plays a dropshot, his partner will move into the forecourt to threaten the net reply. If a pair cannot hit downwards, they will use flat strokes in an attempt to gain the attack. If a pair is forced to lift or clear the shuttlecock, then they must defend: they will adopt a side-by-side position in the rear midcourt, to cover the full width of their court against the opponents' smashes. In doubles, players generally smash to the middle ground between two players in order to take advantage of confusion and clashes.

At high levels of play, the backhand serve has become popular to the extent that forehand serves have become fairly rare at a high level of play. The straight low serve is used most frequently, in an attempt to prevent the opponents gaining the attack immediately. Flick serves are used to prevent the opponent from anticipating the low serve and attacking it decisively.

At high levels of play, doubles rallies are extremely fast. Men's doubles is the most aggressive form of badminton, with a high proportion of powerful jump smashes and very quick reflex exchanges. Because of this, spectator interest is sometimes greater for men's doubles than for singles.

Mixed Doubles

In mixed doubles, both pairs typically try to maintain an attacking formation with the woman at the front and the man at the back. This is because the male players are usually substantially stronger, and can therefore produce smashes that are more powerful. As a result, mixed doubles require greater tactical awareness and subtler positional play. Clever opponents will try to reverse the ideal position, by forcing the woman towards the back or the man towards the front. In order to protect against this danger, mixed players must be careful and systematic in their shot selection.

At high levels of play, the formations will generally be more flexible: the top women players are capable of playing powerfully from the back-court, and will happily do so if required. When the opportunity arises, however, the pair will switch back to the standard mixed attacking position, with the woman in front and men in the back.

Word Bank

stroke	[stroʊk]	n.（打、击等的）一下；（游泳或划船的）划；中风
smash	[smæʃ]	n.& v. 扣球；破碎；冲突
delicate	['delɪkət]	adj. 微妙的；精美的，雅致的；柔和的；易碎的；纤弱的
tumbling	['tʌmblɪŋ]	adj. 翻滚的；歪斜状的
subtle	['sʌtl]	adj. 微妙的；精细的；敏感的
netshot	['netʃɑːt]	n. 网前放小球，网前球
subsequent	['sʌbsɪkwənt]	adj. 后来的，随后的
deception	[dɪ'sepʃn]	n. 欺骗，欺诈；骗术
identical	[aɪ'dentɪkl]	adj. 同一的，完全相同的
slicing	[slaɪsɪŋ]	n. 切断；切片；限制
deceive	[dɪ'siːv]	v. 欺骗，行骗
opponent	[ə'poʊnənt]	n. 对手，反对者，敌手
anticipate	[æn'tɪsɪpeɪt]	v. 预期，期望；占先，抢先；提前使用
momentum	[moʊ'mentəm]	n. 势头；[物] 动量；动力；冲力
shuttlecock	['ʃʌtlkɑːk]	n. 羽毛球；毽子
single	['sɪŋgl]	n.（常用复数）单打比赛；（美）独身者；单程票
exploit	[ɪk'splɔɪt]	v. 利用；开发；剥削；开采
prominent	['prɑːmɪnənt]	adj. 突出的，显著的；杰出的，卓越的
double	['dʌbl]	n.（常用复数）双打
vulnerable	['vʌlnərəbl]	adj. 易受攻击的；易受伤害的；有弱点的
exhausting	[ɪg'zɔːstɪŋ]	adj. 使筋疲力尽的；使耗尽的
conservation	[ˌkɑːnsər'veɪʃn]	n. 保存；保持；保护
forehand	['fɔːrhænd]	n. 正手击球；正手；正拍
flick	[flɪk]	n. 弹开；快速地轻打；轻打声
backhand	['bækhænd]	n. 反手拍；反手抽击
manoeuvring	[mə'nuːvərɪŋ]	n. 部署；调遣；谋略
all-out	[ˌɔːl'aʊt]	adj. 全部的；竭尽全力的；毫无保留的
downwards	['daʊnwərdz]	adv. 向下，往下
arise	[ə'raɪz]	v. 出现；上升；起立
adopt	[ə'dɑːpt]	v. 采取；接受；收养；正式通过
ideal	[aɪ'diːəl]	adj. 理想的；完美的
formation	[fɔːr'meɪʃn]	n. 形成；构造；编队
rearcourt	['rɪəkɔːrt]	n. 后场；后院
intercept	[ˌɪntər'sept]	v. 拦截，截断；窃听

dropshot	['drɑːpˈʃɑːt]	n. 近网短球
forecourt	[ˈfɔːrkɔːrt]	n. 前院；前场
decisively	[dɪˈsaɪsɪvli]	adv. 果断地，决然地
typically	[ˈtɪpɪkli]	adv. 代表性地；作为特色地；通常
substantially	[səbˈstænʃəli]	adv. 实质上；大体上；充分地
reverse	[rɪˈvɜːrs]	v. 颠倒；倒转
systematic	[ˌsɪstəˈmætɪk]	adj. 系统的，体系的，有系统的
flexible	[ˈfleksəbl]	adj. 灵活的；柔韧的；易弯曲的

Phrases

at a premium	非常珍贵；非常需要，渴求
flat strokes	平击球；平抽球
side-by-side position	平行站位
to the extent that...	达到……的程度以致；在这个意义上；在这样的范围内
in an attempt to	力图，试图
flick serve	抖腕弹击发球
mixed doubles	混合双打
tactical awareness	战术意识；场上意识
be capable of	能够……
switch back to	切换回

Critical Reading and Thinking

Read the text and decide whether the following statements are true (T) or false (F).

1. _____ To win in badminton, players need to employ a wide variety of strokes in the right situations.
2. _____ Powerful jumping smashes are more effective than delicate tumbling net returns.
3. _____ Expert players prepare for many different strokes that look almost the same.
4. _____ To force the opponent to move as much as possible, singles strokes are normally directed to the middle of the court.
5. _____ Smashing tends to be more prominent in singles than in doubles.
6. _____ Like the doubles, singles is also a game of all-out aggression.
7. _____ In doubles, both pairs will try to gain and maintain the attack, smashing downwards when the opportunity arises.

8. _____ Spectators are sometimes more interested in men's doubles than in singles.
9. _____ In mixed doubles, both pairs typically try to maintain an attacking formation with the man at the front and the woman at the back.
10. _____ Mixed doubles require greater tactical awareness and subtler positional play.

Translation

Translate the following sentences into Chinese.

1. If the netshot is tight and tumbling, then the opponent's lift will not reach the back of the court, which makes the subsequent smash much harder to return.
2. If an opponent tries to anticipate the stroke, he may move in the wrong direction and may be unable to change his body momentum in time to reach the shuttlecock.
3. Since one person needs to cover the entire court, singles tactics are based on forcing the opponent to move as much as possible.
4. Men's doubles is the most aggressive form of badminton, with a high proportion of powerful jump smashes and very quick reflex exchanges.
5. In mixed doubles, both pairs typically try to maintain an attacking formation with the woman at the front and the man at the back.

Part Three — Listening and Speaking

Task 1

Word Bank

athletic gear		运动装备
rarely	['rerli]	*adv.* 很少；罕有地
cycling	['saɪklɪŋ]	*n.* 骑脚踏车
free of charge		免费，分文不取
awesome	['ɔːsəm]	*adj.* 极好的

Unit 2
Badminton

Listen to two dialogues about badminton and answer the following questions.

1. When will Rose play badminton?
2. Where will they play badminton?
3. What favor does Sam need from Rose?
4. Where did Jenny go yesterday?
5. Does Tom often play badminton? Why?

Task 2

Word Bank

medalist	['medəlɪst]	n. 得到奖牌的人
final	['faɪnl]	n. 决赛
capitalize	['kæpɪtəlaɪz]	v. 利用；使资本化
compatriot	[kəm'peɪtriət]	n. 同胞；同国人
runner-up		（竞赛中的）第二名，亚军
pay tribute to		称赞，歌颂
vociferous	[voʊ'sɪfərəs]	adj. 大声叫喊的
make up for		补偿，弥补
relieved	[rɪ'liːvd]	adj. 宽慰的；放心的

Listen to a news report about badminton and fill in the blanks with the information you hear.

Indonesia's Tontowi Ahmad and Liliyana Natsir became badminton's first gold 1._____ of Rio 2016 when they 2._____ Malaysia's Chan Peng Soon and Goh Liu Ying 21-14, 21-12 in the 3._____. Having 4._____ Zhang Nan and Zhao Yunlei of China in the semis, the Indonesian pair 5._____ on their opponent's 6._____ and produced some quality play of their own to go one better than the 7._____ they won at Beijing 8._____. The 9._____ went to China's Zhang Nan and Zhao Yunlei, who defeated 10._____ and London 2012 runners-up Xu Chen and Ma Jin 21-7, 21-11.

Task 3

Listen to the five sentences from the recording, repeat each sentence after it is spoken, and then write it down.

1. _____.
2. _____.

35

3. _____.
4. _____.
5. _____.

Task 4

Discuss the following questions in your group.

1. Who is your favorite badminton player? Why do you like him or her?
2. Do you like Chinese badminton player Lin Dan? Why or why not?

Part Four Writing

Complaint Letters

    A complaint letter is usually written to complain about the goods you have bought or the service you have received. Keep it short and to the point to help ensure that your letter will be read in its entirety.

    In the first paragraph you should clearly express what the problem is and any relevant information such as the date/time of the issue, location, name of the product, the specific problem with the purchase and price or the services you have received.

    The next paragraph should state how you would like the problem to be solved. It may be a request of an apology for poor services, of an exchange of the malfunctioned product, or of a refund.

    The last paragraph should thank the reader for the time and show your expectation of a quick reply to solve the problem reasonably.

    You should include your telephone number/e-mail address after your printed name so that the reader can contact you as soon as possible if necessary.

Sample

Allan Donald
154 Cliffside Drive
Davenport, NY 13750
Jun 9, 2014

The Customer Relationship Manager
Westside World Enterprise
173 Hillcrest Avenue
Boston, MA 02110

Dear Sir/Madam,

This is to inform that I am amongst the regular customer of your store and I was very much satisfied with the services you were providing to your guests. But today I would like to bring your attention to the poor service that I received from one of your staff at your Boston chain-store last Friday.

I was at your store regarding some information about the product for my tennis training. Then I came across with one of your staff who must be around twenty years of age. I asked him about my query with all the desired details of that particular product. Then he replied me, "Sir, please wait for a moment and I will get back to you shortly." But nobody turned out in the following 20 minutes. I could not get his name as there was no name tag on his uniform. When I tried to enquire the same with another person, he replied, "This is none of my business." As whole I was not supported with any of the staff of yours, which was very much disgusting for me.

I am very upset with the improper training strategies of your employees to attend the customers and let me tell you honestly that it might affect negatively your customer's trust from your store. I sincerely hope you can make an apology to me and please choose your staff wisely to offer your customers service well for the long haul.

Yours sincerely,

Allan Donald

Allan Donald

Adapted from http://www.lettersfree.com/complaint-letter-for-poor-service/

Follow-up Writing

You have bought a new tennis racket from the Internet lately. But when you received the product, you found a small tear on the package box, and a broken string on the racket. Write a letter to complain about the purchase and ask for a refund. You can use the following information as the beginning.

65 Market Street

Val Haven, CT 95135

June 24, 2016

Customer Service

Cool Sports, LLC

8423 Green Terrace Road

Oysterville, WA 65435

Dear Sir or Madam,

Part One — Knowledge Preparation

Running is regularly enjoyed by millions of people because it's both good for health and easy to start. All you really need is a good pair of running shoes and the willingness to get started. Running seems so simple that preparing to start a running routine may sound silly. But learning more about proper running forms, how running can help you reach your health goals, how to stay well while running and more can go a long way in helping you get the most of your new habit.

The majority of people participate in the running for the physical, mental, and social benefits it brings. Casual runners usually love the accessibility of running—you don't need any fancy equipment, it's relatively inexpensive, and you can do it almost anywhere. It's never too late to start running, as many people who have taken up the sport start this activity in their 50s, 60s, and even 70s.

跑步之所以能被无数人有规律地坚持着，是因为它不仅对人的身体有好处，而且人们很容易开始这项运动。你需要的只是一双合适的跑鞋和打算开始的决心。跑步似乎太简单了，所以制定跑步计划似乎显得太滑稽。但事实上，了解更适当的跑步形式、跑步如何能帮你达到健康目标、跑步时如何保持良好的状态以及更多的跑步知识则会帮助你养成新的好习惯。

大多数人加入跑步运动，因为它对身体、心理和社会交际都有好处。跑步的"门槛很低"——不需要任何高大上的设备，相对比较经济实惠，而且几乎在任何地方都可以进行。跑步也没有年龄限制，任何年纪都可以开始这项运动，很多人50多岁、60多岁，甚至70多岁才开始跑步运动。

Unit 3
Running and Jogging

Part Two Reading

 Text A

Jogging

1 The word "jog", originating in England in the mid-16th century, was often used in English and North American literature to describe short quick movements, either intentional or unintentional. Jogging is a form of running at a slow or leisurely pace. The main intention is to increase physical fitness with less stress on the body than from faster running, or to maintain a steady speed for longer periods of time. Performed over long distances, it is a form of aerobic endurance training.

2 Once in the United States jogging was called "roadwork" when athletes in training customarily ran several miles each day as part of their conditioning. But now jogging has become one of the most popular individual sports in the world. Many theories, even some mystical ones, have been advanced to explain the popularity of jogging. The plain truth is that jogging is a cheap, quick and efficient way to maintain physical fitness.

3 Only one sort of equipment is needed—a pair of good shoes. Physicians advise beginning joggers not to try to run in tennis or gym shoes. Many design advances have been made in only the last several years that make a pair of excellent running shoes indispensable if a runner wishes to develop as quickly as possible, with as little chance of injury as possible. A pair of good running shoes will have soft pads for absorbing shock, as well as slightly built-up heels and full heel cups that will give the knee and ankle more stability. A wise investment in good shoes will prevent blisters and the foot, ankle and knee injuries, and will also enable the wearer to run on paved or soft surfaces. No other special equipment is needed; you can jog in any clothing you desire, even your street clothes.

4 According to a study by Stanford University School of Medicine, jogging is effective in increasing human lifespan, and decreasing the effects of aging, with benefits for the cardiovascular system. Jogging is useful for fighting obesity and staying healthy. The National Cancer Institute has performed studies that suggest jogging and other types of aerobic exercise can reduce the risk of lung, colon, breast and prostate cancers. It is suggested by the American Cancer Society that jogging for at least 30 minutes five days a week can help in cancer prevention.

5 The most useful sort of exercise is the one that develops the heart, lungs, and circulatory systems. One can train more specifically, as by developing strength for weight lifting or the ability

41

to run straight ahead for short distances with great power as in football, but running trains your heart and lungs to deliver oxygen more efficiently to all parts of your body. It is worth doing that: this sort of exercise is the only kind that can reduce heart disease.

6 While jogging on a treadmill will provide health benefits, such as cancer prevention, and aid in weight loss, jogging outdoors can have the additional benefits of increased energy and concentration. Jogging outdoors is a better way to improve energy levels and advance mood than using a treadmill at the gym. Jogging also prevents muscle and bone damage that often occurs with age, improves heart performance and blood circulation and assists in preserving a balanced weight gain.

7 The optimal amount of jogging per week was 1 to 2.4 hours, the optimal frequency was 2–3 times per week, and the optimal speed was "slow" or "average".

Word Bank

originate	[əˈrɪdʒɪneɪt]	v. 发源；发生
intentional	[ɪnˈtenʃənl]	adj. 故意的，蓄意的；策划的
leisurely	[ˈliːʒərli]	adj. 悠闲的，从容的
steady	[ˈstedi]	adj. 稳定的；不变的；沉着的
aerobic	[eˈroʊbɪk]	adj. 需氧的；有氧健身的
endurance	[ɪnˈdʊrəns]	n. 忍耐力；忍耐；持久
customarily	[ˌkʌstəˈmerəli]	adv. 通常，习惯上
conditioning	[kənˈdɪʃənɪŋ]	n. 调节；条件；训练，健身训练
individual	[ˌɪndɪˈvɪdʒuəl]	adj. 个人的；个别的；独特的
mystical	[ˈmɪstɪkl]	adj. 神秘的；神秘主义的
efficient	[ɪˈfɪʃnt]	adj. 有效率的；有能力的；生效的
physician	[fɪˈzɪʃn]	n. [医] 医师，内科医师
indispensable	[ˌɪndɪˈspensəbl]	adj. 不可缺少的，绝对必要的；责无旁贷的
pad	[pæd]	n. 衬垫；护具
absorb	[əbˈzɔːrb]	v. 吸收；吸引；承受
slightly	[ˈslaɪtli]	adv. 些微地，轻微地；纤细地
heel	[hiːl]	n. 脚后跟，踵
ankle	[ˈæŋkl]	n. 踝关节，踝
stability	[stəˈbɪləti]	n. 稳定性；坚定，恒心
blister	[ˈblɪstər]	n. 水疱
lifespan	[ˈlaɪfspæn]	n. 寿命
cardiovascular	[ˌkɑːrdioʊˈvæskjələr]	adj. [解剖] 心血管的
obesity	[oʊˈbiːsəti]	n. 肥大，肥胖

colon	[ˈkoʊlən]	n.	［解剖］结肠
prostate	[ˈprɑːsteɪt]	n.	［解剖］前列腺
circulatory	[ˈsɜːrkjələtɔːri]	adj.	循环的
oxygen	[ˈɑːksɪdʒən]	n.	［化学］氧气
treadmill	[ˈtredmɪl]	n.	跑步机
additional	[əˈdɪʃənl]	adj.	附加的，额外的
concentration	[ˌkɑːnsnˈtreɪʃn]	n.	集中；专心
assist	[əˈsɪst]	v.	帮助；促进
optimal	[ˈɑːptɪməl]	adj.	最佳的，最理想的
frequency	[ˈfriːkwənsi]	n.	频率；频繁

Phrases

heel cups	后跟垫
aerobic exercise	有氧运动
weight lifting	举重
short distance	短距离，短程
be worth doing	值得做……

Task 1 Text Organization

Read the text and fill in the blanks.

Paragraphs	Key Words	Supporting Details
Paras. 1–2	_____ to jogging	• the _____ of the word "jog" • the _____ of "jogging" • Jogging has become _____ in the world.
Para. 3	_____ for jogging	• a pair of _____
Paras. 4-6	_____ of jogging	• Jogging is effective in increasing _____, decreasing _____, and preventing _____. • Jogging is the only kind of exercise that can _____. • Jogging outdoors is a better way to _____.

| Para. 7 | _____ on jogging | • optimal amount: _____
• optimal frequency: _____
• optimal speed: _____ |

Task 2 Reading Comprehension

Exercise 1

Read the text and decide whether the following statements are true (T) or false (F).

1. _____ Jogging is popular because it is a form of aerobic endurance training.
2. _____ Clothes and shoes are important to jogging.
3. _____ Jogging is effective in keeping fit.
4. _____ If one's heart, lungs and circulatory systems work well, the body will be in good conditions for sports, work or emergencies.
5. _____ Jogging on a treadmill will provide more benefits than jogging outdoors.

Exercise 2

Read the text and answer the following questions.

1. What's the meaning of the word "jog" in English and North American literature?
2. What does a pair of good running shoes really mean?
3. What does the study of Stanford University School of Medicine demonstrate?
4. What is the most useful sort of exercise?
5. Does jogging on a treadmill and jogging outdoors have the same effect?

Task 3 Language in Use

Exercise 1

Match the underlined words in the left column with their corresponding meanings in the right column.

1. The word "jog" originated in England in the mid-16th century.
2. The main intention is to maintain a steady speed for longer periods of time.
3. Athletes in training customarily ran several miles each day as part of their conditioning.

A. of hidden meaning or spiritual power

B. absolutely necessary; essential

C. came into existence; took on form or shape

4. Many theories, even some <u>mystical</u> ones, have been advanced to explain the popularity of jogging.

5. Jogging is a cheap, quick and <u>efficient</u> way to maintain physical fitness.

6. A pair of excellent running shoes will be <u>indispensable</u> if a runner wishes to develop as quickly as possible.

7. A pair of good running shoes will have soft pads for <u>absorbing</u> shock.

8. A wise <u>investment</u> in good shoes will prevent blisters.

9. You can jog in any clothing you <u>desire</u>, even your street clothes.

10. The <u>optimal</u> amount per week was 1 to 2.4 hours.

D. expect and wish; want strongly

E. even and regular

F. money that is invested with an expectation of profit

G. by custom; according to common practice

H. effective without wasting time or effort or expense

I. most desirable; best

J. taking in; reducing the effect of

Exercise 2

Select one word or phase for each blank from a list of choices given below and fill in the blank with its correct form.

| suggest | decrease | worth | obesity | circulatory system |
| prevent | efficient | effect | aerobic exercise | specific |

According to a study by Stanford University School of Medicine, jogging is **1.**_____ in increasing human lifespan, and **2.**_____ the effects of aging, with benefits for the cardiovascular system. Jogging is useful for fighting **3.**_____ and staying healthy. The National Cancer Institute has performed studies that **4.**_____ jogging and other types of **5.**_____ can reduce the risk of lung, colon, breast and prostate cancers. It is suggested by the American Cancer Society that jogging for at least 30 minutes five days a week can help in cancer **6.**_____.

The most useful sort of exercise is the one that develops the heart, lungs, and **7.**_____. One can train more **8.**_____, as by developing strength for weight lifting or the ability to run straight ahead for short distances with great power as in football, but running trains your heart and lungs to deliver oxygen more **9.**_____ to all parts of your body. It is **10.**_____ doing that: this sort of exercise is the only kind that can reduce heart disease.

Exercise 3

Translate the following sentences into English.

1. 慢跑是一种缓慢休闲的运动形式。(jogging)
2. 运动使人延年益寿、抵抗衰老。(increase human lifespan)
3. 要提高跑步速度且能减少受伤的可能性,一双不错的跑鞋是必不可少的。(indispensable)
4. 最有效的运动是加强心、肺和循环系统功能的运动。(circulatory system)
5. 与室内运动相比,户外慢跑有诸多好处,如预防癌症和减肥等。(cancer prevention)

Running for Weight Loss

Christine Luff

As one of the most vigorous exercises out there, running is an extremely efficient activity for weight loss. Many runners drop pounds and are able to maintain their weight. However, it is worth noting that others fall victim to common weight loss mistakes. If you're hoping to use running to lose weight, heeding some tried and true advice can help you be successful and stay on track.

Healthy Eating Is the First Step

If you want to lose weight by running, keep in mind that you'll only shed pounds if you burn more calories than you consume. To lose a pound, you have to burn, through exercise or life functions, about 3,500 calories. So, you'll need to combine running with a healthy diet. Runners have special nutrition needs, but the basic principles for healthy eating still apply. Try choosing smaller portions of high-fat and high-calorie foods and eating more whole grains, fruits, and vegetables.

One common eating mistake among runners is that they overcompensate for the calories burned by exercise with extra calories from more food and beverages. Some runners even find that they gain weight or hit a weight loss wall, despite their regular training.

One way to prevent "stealth calorie" consumption or mindless eating is to write everything you're eating in a journal for a few weeks. Reviewing a record of your food intake will help you see where your diet needs improvement. Runners often find that they constantly feel hungry, so you'll want to try to plan your snacks and meals to avoid going overboard.

Follow a Training Schedule

Sticking to a training schedule is a simple way to stay motivated to run. You'll know exactly what you need to do every day, and it will be harder to postpone or skip workouts. Following a schedule can also help you avoid a running injury by not increasing your mileage too quickly.

Unit 3
Running and Jogging

Run Regularly

Consistency is the key, according to runners who successfully lose weight and keep it off. If you don't want to follow a schedule, you still need to make sure you're running regularly because you won't lose weight by running once a week. It's best to get some activities every day. But if that's not possible, try to shoot for at least three to four times per week. If you find that your motivation to run is suffering, follow these tips to get inspired. One trick to staying motivated is to give yourself little rewards when you reach a milestone, such as running a specific race or reaching a certain distance. Just make sure that you use non-food rewards, such as a pedicure, massage, or cool running gear.

Running is a great activity for weight loss. It has a high calorie burn and can be done anywhere with nothing more needed than a good pair of sneakers. If you find that running is not for you, don't give up on your weight loss efforts. Find an exercise that you enjoy. It's more important that you are able to stick with your routine than to choose one particular activity over another.

Word Bank

vigorous	['vɪgərəs]	adj. 有力的；精力充沛的
heed	[hiːd]	v. 注意，留心
shed	[ʃed]	v. 摆脱
nutrition	[nuˈtrɪʃn]	n. 营养；营养学；营养品
principle	[ˈprɪnsəpl]	n. 原则；法则
apply	[əˈplaɪ]	v. 申请；适用
portion	[ˈpɔːrʃn]	n. 部分
overcompensate	[ˌoʊvərˈkɑːmpenseɪt]	v. 过度补偿
beverage	[ˈbevərɪdʒ]	n. 饮料
despite	[dɪˈspaɪt]	prep. 尽管，不管
stealth	[stelθ]	n. 秘密；隐蔽
constantly	[ˈkɑːnstəntli]	adv. 不断地；时常地
snack	[snæk]	n. 小吃；快餐；零食
schedule	[ˈskedʒuːl]	n. 时间表；计划表
motivate	[ˈmoʊtɪveɪt]	v. 使有动机，激发……的积极性
postpone	[poʊˈspoʊn]	v. 使……延期
skip	[skɪp]	v. 跳过；遗漏
mileage	[ˈmaɪlɪdʒ]	n. 英里数
consistency	[kənˈsɪstənsi]	n. 坚持；一致性
suffering	[ˈsʌfərɪŋ]	n. 受难；苦楚

milestone	['maɪlstoʊn]	n. 里程碑
pedicure	['pedɪkjʊr]	n. 修趾甲术；足部护理
massage	[mə'sɑːʒ]	n. 按摩；揉
sneaker	['sniːkər]	n. 运动鞋

Phrases

fall victim to	成为……的牺牲品；成为……的受害者
stay on track	走上正轨
combine with	与……结合
hit a wall	碰壁
go overboard	过火；鲁莽从事
stick to	坚持

Critical Reading and Thinking

Read the text and decide whether the following statements are true (T) or false (F).

1. _____ Many runners can succeed in losing weight.
2. _____ A healthy diet is essential if you want to lose weight by running.
3. _____ Runners have special nutrition needs, so they should choose high-fat and high-calorie foods.
4. _____ With calories burned by exercise, runners have to get extra calories from more food and beverages.
5. _____ Although some runners go on with regular training, they fail in losing weight.
6. _____ Runners often feel hungry, so they should eat what they want without planning.
7. _____ Sticking to a training schedule can make you keep motivation in running and avoid a running injury.
8. _____ If you don't want to run regularly, you will also lose weight by running once a week.
9. _____ Give yourself some delicious food rewards when you reach a certain distance.
10. _____ Being able to follow the schedule is more important than to decide what activity should be chosen.

Translation

Translate the following sentences into Chinese.

1. As one of the most vigorous exercises out there, running is an extremely efficient activity for weight loss.
2. Try choosing smaller portions of high-fat and high-calorie foods and eating more whole grains, fruits, and vegetables.
3. Runners often find that they constantly feel hungry, so you'll want to try to plan your snacks and meals to avoid going overboard.
4. If you don't want to follow a schedule, you still need to make sure you're running regularly because you won't lose weight by running once a week.
5. It's more important that you are able to stick with your routine than to choose one particular activity over another.

Part Three — Listening and Speaking

Task 1

Word Bank

scenery	[ˈsiːnəri]	n.	风景；景色
chest	[tʃest]	n.	胸部，胸腔
rust	[rʌst]	v.	（使）生锈
flexibility	[ˌfleksəˈbɪləti]	n.	柔度，柔韧性；机动性，灵活性

Listen to a conversation about jogging and answer the following questions.

1. What does Lisa suggest?
2. Is Daniel willing to go jogging at first?
3. What is the benefit of jogging?
4. What is the benefit of swimming?

Task 2

Word Bank

trot	[trɑːt]	v. 小跑
fitness	['fɪtnəs]	n. 健康；适当，适合
high-impact		（锻炼）高强度的
place strain on		使……（极度）紧张，使处于紧张状态
joint	[dʒɔɪnt]	n. 关节
stair climbing		爬楼梯
recovery	[rɪ'kʌvəri]	n. 恢复，复原
interval	['ɪntəvl]	n. 间隔
lap	[læp]	n. 一圈跑道

Listen to the news report about jogging and fill in the blanks with the information you hear.

Jogging is a form of **1.**_____ or running at a slow or **2.**_____ pace. The main **3.**_____ is to increase fitness without stress. Jogging is a "**4.**_____" exercise that places **5.**_____ on the body, notably the **6.**_____ of the knee. This is actually one of the basic reasons for doing the exercise, as the impact drives **7.**_____ processes in the areas of the body stressed by that impact. Some people drop jogging in order to take up "lower-impact" exercises such as **8.**_____, swimming or cycling.

Jogging is often used by serious runners as a means of **9.**_____ recovery during interval training. The runner who may just have completed a fast 400-metre repetition at a sub-5-minute mile **10.**_____, may drop to an 8-minute mile pace for a recovery lap.

Task 3

Listen to the five sentences from the recording, repeat each sentence after it is spoken, and then write it down.

1. _____.
2. _____.
3. _____.
4. _____.
5. _____.

Task 4

Discuss the following questions in your group.

1. What is your favorite sport? Why do you like that sport?
2. Give a presentation on the reasons why people like jogging.

Apology Letters

Apology letters are written after mistakes cause offense or even loss to others. While most of time apologizing in person is recommended, there are also situations in which written apology may be more preferable. To write an apology letter, you'll need to express your apology directly in the beginning. Then acknowledge full responsibility for your part in the matter by stating clearly and specifically what happened and what you are sorry for. You should also mention the solution to show your sincerity and provide reassurance to the offended person. At last, end the letter with your apology to reinforce your genuine regret. You may also express your openness to discuss what happened to make the letter more effective. Apology letters may vary greatly in tone since they may either be in a business style (Sample 1) or a personal style (Sample 2).

Sample 1

Customer Service

Cool Sports, LLC

8423 Green Terrace Road

Oysterville, WA 65435

June 30, 2016

Ken Thomas

65 Market Street

Val Haven, CT 95135

Dear Mr. Thomas,

I apologize for the problem of order CG77924190. We have just changed a new logistics company which may not have packed our products in proper ways, but we did communicate with them the issue and they have promised to make improvement in their packing. Surely we will refund the money to your account within three days. And for your trouble, we have enclosed a $25 gift certificate which can be used at any of our stores. Once again I would like to apologize for the dissatisfaction we have brought to you and any inconveniences this may have caused you.

Sincerely,

Scott Mahoney

Scott Mahoney

Customer Service Manager

Sample 2

23 Pine Zaggat Lane

Hamperville, NE 53792

January 7, 2015

Dear Joseph,

    Please accept my sincere apology for missing our jogging date yesterday. In the middle of the rush to meet our printing deadline, I overlooked our appointment. Could we make another date for the next week? I enjoy our time together and it gives me a much-needed break from the stress here at the office. Let's meet at Starbucks at noon next Tuesday; it will be my treat.

Your friend,

Michael

Michael

Follow-up Writing

You had a breakfast date with your fried Jolene today, but you jogged too long and forgot the date. Write an apology letter to Jolene, and invite her to a meal at the new Chinese restaurant Oriental Tastes.

Unit 4
Leisure Sports

Part One — Knowledge Preparation

"Golf" is the transliteration of "Kolf" in Dutch. It originally means a good life in the green and fresh air. We can know the meaning from the word "golf": G—green, O—oxygen, L—light and F—friendship. Now golf has been gradually going global and become a fashion sport which integrates fitness, entertainment and athletics. Golf professionalization has been well developed in the world and gradually formed professional tour events headed by the PGA Championship, as well as the four Grand Slams, the Ryder Cup, the President Cup, and many other tournaments. The four Grand Slams events include the American Masters, the US Open Championship, the British Open Championship, and the PGA Tournament. It can be said that golf is one of the sports whose professionalization has developed well in the world.

"高尔夫"是荷兰文"Kolf"的音译，原意为"在绿地和新鲜空气中的美好生活"。这从高尔夫球的英文单词GOLF可以看出来：G代表"绿色"；O代表"氧气"；L代表"阳光"；F代表"友谊"。高尔夫球已经成为一项全球性的体育运动，也是一项集健康、休闲与健身于一体的运动项目。当今，国际高尔夫的职业化程度已经十分发达，形成了以美巡赛为首的职业巡回赛，具有四大满贯赛、莱德杯、总统杯及其他等知名的赛事。四大满贯赛事包括美国大师赛、美国公开赛、英国公开赛和PGA巡回赛。高尔夫可以说是国际上职业化开展较好的运动项目之一。

Part Two — Reading

Chinese Golf—Chuiwan

1. Chuiwan was a ball game in ancient China. Players used a rod or stick to drive the ball into holes on the ground in very much the same way as the modern game of golf. During the reign of Yuan Shizu in the Yuan dynasty in 1282, a book called *The Classic of Ball* was published,, with a perfect description about the course, instruments, the number of competitors, umpire and the

counting of Chuiwan. The book was divided into two parts. It says: the course of Chuiwan is a garden with rough terrain and a wide field of vision. Then choose a spacious place to decide the one-chi-squared ball-base after the location of the course. A number of holes are dug 60 or 100 steps away from the base. Beside each of the base a small colored banner is set. The instruments of Chuiwan are rods and a ball. The end of the rod should be curved in order to hit the ball well. When the competition begins, players hit the ball in turn. If the player hits the ball into the hole in three hits, he will get a chip; if fouls, he will be punished a chip.

2 Chuiwan is generally divided into the Greatest, the Middle and the Smallest sports according to the numbers of the players. Usually the player should gain 20 chips in one match in the Greatest sport, 15 chips in the Middle, ten in the Smallest. Chuiwan and golf have extreme similarities, which indicates the two should have certain historical connections.

3 It is recorded that Chuiwan originated from the Stick-and-Goal game in the Tang dynasty, which is similar to the modern hockey. It developed into Chuiwan in the Song dynasty, matured in the 12th century and came to its summit in Song, Yuan and Ming dynasties, but it suddenly disappeared at the end of the Ming dynasty and the beginning of the Qing dynasty. During the later years of the 19th century, when golf was introduced into China, it was regarded as a new and strange sport of the western society. However, concerning the history of golf, *Japan Sports Dictionary* says: it was thought to start in the Great Britain, but a drawing of golf was discovered on a china in Holland recently. And according to the research, golf originated in Holland in the early years of the 15th century. Therefore, golf must be at least three centuries later than Chinese Chuiwan. Compared with the rich certificates and pictures of Chinese Chuiwan, the proofs about the origin of golf are rare, only a picture on a china reminding us of the important and significant event happened in the 13th century—the Mongolians invaded Europe. The Mongolians went on the expeditions twice to the West during the years of 1219–1242 AD, when they introduced the paper-making, compass and gunpowder, etc. into Europe.

4 Hence, we can deduce the Eastern civilization—Chuiwan, was introduced into Europe and evolved to the present game of golf in the confrontation and combination of the East and the West.

Word Bank

reign	[reɪn]	*n.*	君主的统治；君主统治时期
competitor	[kəmˈpetɪtər]	*n.*	竞争者；对手
umpire	[ˈʌmpaɪər]	*n.*	裁判员；仲裁人
counting	[kaʊntɪŋ]	*n.*	计算
terrain	[təˈreɪn]	*n.*	地形，地势；地面，地带
vision	[ˈvɪʒn]	*n.*	视力，视觉；美景

curve	[kɜːrv]	v. 使弯曲；使成曲线
foul	[faʊl]	v. [体] 违反规则
chip	[tʃɪp]	n. 筹码
similarity	[ˌsɪməˈlærəti]	n. 类似；相像性，相仿性
mature	[məˈtʃʊr]	adj. 成熟的；仔细考虑过的
summit	[ˈsʌmɪt]	n. 顶峰；高层会议；最高阶层
certificate	[sərˈtɪfɪkət]	n. 证明书；文凭，结业证书
expedition	[ˌekspəˈdɪʃn]	n. 远航；考察队，远征军
deduce	[dɪˈduːs]	v. 演绎；推论，推断；追溯根源
confrontation	[ˌkɑːnfrənˈteɪʃn]	n. 对抗，对峙；面对；遭遇

Phrases

divide into	分成，分为
originate from	起源；来自……，源于……
be similar to	相似于
compared with	与……比较，与……相比
remind sb. of sth.	提醒某人某事

Task 1 Text Organization

Read the text and fill in the blanks.

Paragraphs	Key Words	Supporting Details
Para. 1	The description of Chuiwan	• Chuiwan is to _____ with the rod or stick. • The course of Chuiwan is _____ with _____ and a wide field of _____. • A number of _____ are _____ 60 or 100 steps away from the base. • Beside each of the base _____ is set. • When the competition begins, players _____ _____.

Paras. 2-3	The division of Chuiwan and the history of golf	• Chuiwan is divided into _____ _____ according to the _____ of players. • Chuiwan _____ from the Stick-and Goal game in the _____ dynasty, _____ into Chuiwan in the Song dynasty, _____ in the 12th century and came to _____ in Song, Yuan and Ming dynasties. • According to *Japan Sports Dictionary*, golf was thought to start in the _____, but a _____ was discovered on a china in Holland. From the drawing, people deduced the origin of golf in Holland was in the early years of the _____ century. • Thus golf must be _____ later than Chinese Chuiwan.
Para. 4	Conclusion	• Chuiwan was brought into _____ and _____ to the present game of golf through the invasion of Mongolians in Europe.

Task 2 Reading Comprehension

Exercise 1

Read the text and decide whether the following statements are true (T) or false (F).

1. _____ Players will be punished a chip if they haven't hit the ball.
2. _____ There are fewer similarities between Chinese Chuiwan and golf.
3. _____ When golf was introduced into China, it was immediately thought to be connected with Chuiwan.
4. _____ There was not much evidence to prove the origin of golf in the western world.
5. _____ According to the text, Chuiwan was the base of the modern golf.

Exercise 2

Read the text and answer the following questions.

1. Can you describe the course of Chuiwan in details?
2. What are the rules of Chuiwan?
3. How is Chuiwan divided?
4. From what aspects can we conclude that Chuiwan and golf have extreme similarities?
5. What event happened in the 13th century can we deduce that modern golf is the evolution of Chuiwan?

Task 3 Language in Use

Exercise 1

Match the underlined words or phrase in the left column with their corresponding meanings in the right column.

1. A pen is an <u>instrument</u> used in writing with ink.
2. He has denied any <u>connection</u> to the bombing.
3. Due to limited space, we cannot <u>publish</u> all the messages received.
4. In the city squares the neon lights flashed <u>in turn</u>.
5. The government has <u>introduced</u> a number of other money-saving moves.
6. They talked about the competing theories of the <u>origin</u> of life.
7. He expected to <u>deduce</u> new ideas by mathematical means.
8. Critical thinking represents the <u>combination</u> of education, experience, and research.
9. The ball <u>curved</u> strangely in the air.
10. The <u>similarities</u> between Mars and Earth were enough to keep alive hopes of some form of Martian life.

A. prepare and issue for public distribution or sale
B. brought something new to an environment
C. an event that is a beginning
D. the act of bringing two things into contact
E. conclude by reasoning
F. the act of combining things to form a new whole
G. formed an arch
H. a small tool
I. in proper order or sequence
J. the qualities of being similar

Unit 4
Leisure Sports

Exercise 2

Select one word for each blank from a list of choices given below and fill in the blank with its correct form.

| concern | similarity | combine | deduce | mature |
| confront | originate | record | connect | similar |

China has contributed the paper-making, compass, gunpowder, etc. to the world. Now it has **1.**_____ to show Chuiwan and golf have some **2.**_____, which tells us the two should have certain historical **3.**_____. **4.**_____ the history of golf, there were two versions. One was said to start in the Great Britain. Another was said to be **5.**_____ in Holland in the early years of the 15th century. But the Stick-and-Goal game, which is **6.**_____ to the modern hockey, developed into Chuiwan in the Song dynasty, **7.**_____ in the 12th century and came to its summit in Song, Yuan and Ming dynasties. Hence, we can **8.**_____ golf must be at least three centuries later than Chinese Chuiwan. Chuiwan was brought into Europe and developed to the current golf in the **9.**_____ and **10.**_____ of the East and the West by Mongolians.

Exercise 3

Translate the following sentences into English.
1. 学生被分为两个大组进行比赛。(divide into)
2. 任何理论都来源于实践，反过来为实践服务。(originate from)
3. 这个示例与前一个示例相似。(be similar to)
4. 个人的力量和群众的力量相比，不过是沧海一粟。(compared with)
5. 你说这样的话，使我想起了你的父亲。(remind sb. of sth.)

Text B

Sport Climbing Set to Be Olympic Sport for Tokyo 2020

16 July 2016

Sport climbing is confirmed as a new Olympic sport for the Tokyo 2020 Games. An International Olympic Committee (IOC) session announced on August 3rd that the sport will be added to the program for four years' time.

The sport climbing event, as it's being called by the IOC, will combine three traditionally separate climbing events—bouldering, sport climbing, and speed climbing—into a single

59

competition. It is one of five sports put forward by Tokyo organizers, a proposal backed unanimously by the IOC executive board. Skateboarding, surfing, karate and baseball/softball also became Olympic sports at the meeting. Over the past two decades, each of them has grown in popularity, participation, and public awareness.

IOC President Thomas Bach said, "We want to take sport to the youth. With the many options that young people have, we cannot expect any more that they will come automatically to us. We have to go to them. The five sports are an innovative combination of established and emerging, youth-focused events that are popular in Japan and will add to the legacy of the Tokyo Games."

Future Games hosts are being given a chance to bring in one or more sports popular in their country to boost ratings and attract greater sponsorship. The event program for the existing 28 Olympic sports—which includes golf as it returns this year for the first time since 1904—will be finalized in mid-2017.

More than 20 male golfers, including the top four in the world, have pulled out of this summer's Games, with many citing concern over the Zika virus—a mosquito-borne virus linked to brain defects in newborn babies. IOC president Thomas Bach said this week that the absences would be considered when the Tokyo 2020 line-up is decided.

The five new sports "offer a key focus on youth", the IOC has previously said, have a "significant popularity in Japan and beyond", and would be the "most comprehensive evolution of the Olympic program in modern history". The inclusion of the five new sports will add 18 events and 474 athletes—with an equal number of male and female participants—to the Tokyo Games. None of the 28 traditional Olympic sports, including golf, will be affected by this addition. Among climbers, surfers, and skateboarders, the reaction has been mixed. Many see the Olympics' acceptance as an affront to the countercultural roots that they consider inherent to their sports.

Sport climbing involves participants scaling permanent anchors, like bolts, fixed to the rock. According to the International Federation of Sport Climbing, more than 140 countries have climbing walls, with 35 million climbers around the world. The average age is 23 years old, with 40% under 20.

Great Britain's Shauna Coxsey, the Bouldering World Cup champion, told *The Guardian*: "This will make climbing even more popular and hopefully open it up to people who normally would not give it a go." Rob Adie, competitions officer at the British Mountaineering Council, which has helped campaign for climbing to be made an Olympic sport, said: "Climbing is such a wide-ranging sport and there are so many different facets. It is a good thing that it will be recognized on a world stage."

Unit 4
Leisure Sports

Word Bank

confirm	[kən'fɜːrm]	v. 证实；批准；确定
session	['seʃn]	n. 会议；会期；开庭期；学期；一段时间
unanimously	[juˈnænɪməsli]	adv. 全体一致地，无异议地
boost	[buːst]	v. 提高，增加；鼓励；举起；为……做宣传
sponsorship	[ˈspɑːnsərʃɪp]	n. 赞助；倡议；保证人地位
defect	[ˈdiːfekt]	n. 缺点；缺陷
evolution	[ˌiːvəˈluːʃn]	n. 进化；发展；演变
mountaineering	[ˌmaʊntnˈɪrɪŋ]	n. 登山运动，爬山
campaign	[kæmˈpeɪn]	v. 参加竞选；从事运动
facet	[ˈfæsɪt]	n. 小平面；方面

Phrases

pull out	v. 拔出；离开，出发，起程；恢复健康；逃避责任；背约
line-up	n. 一排人或物（亦作 lineup） v. 排成行；排成直线

Proper Name

The Guardian	英国《卫报》

Critical Reading and Thinking

Read the text and decide whether the following statements are true (T) or false (F).

1. _____ The five sports which will be added into 2020 Tokyo Olympics are sport climbing, surfing, skateboarding, skiing and baseball.

2. _____ IOC is set to announce on 3 August that the sport will be added to the program for four years.

3. _____ Everyone on executive board agreed with the proposal to add sport climbing into Olympic sports events.

4. _____ Golf was featured in the Olympic Games in mid-2007.

5. _____ There are 28 Olympic sports since 1904.

6. _____ Future Games hosts can bring in one or more sport which is popular in the country into the Olympics.

7. _____ The IOC President Thomas Bach said the athletes who gave up this summer Olympics may run the risk of not attending the Tokyo Olympics.

8. _____ The IOC said the five new sports offer a new focus on youth.

9. _____ Shauna Coxsey, the Bouldering World Cup champion, said the new change will close the door to those who are not dedicated to the sports.

10. _____ Rob Adie claimed that climbing is a wide-ranging sport and there are many different facets.

Translation

Translate the following sentences into Chinese.

1. An International Olympic Committee (IOC) session is set to announce on 3 August that the sport will be added to the program for four years' time.

2. Future Games hosts are being given a chance to bring in one or more sports popular in their country to boost ratings and attract greater sponsorship.

3. The five new sports "offer a key focus on youth", the IOC has previously said, have a "significant popularity in Japan and beyond", and would be the "most comprehensive evolution of the Olympic program in modern history".

4. More than 20 male golfers, including the top four in the world, have pulled out of this summer's Games, with many citing concern over the Zika virus—a mosquito-borne virus linked to brain defects in newborn babies.

5. This will make climbing even more popular and hopefully open it up to people who normally wouldn't give it a go.

Part Three Listening and Speaking

Task 1

Word Bank

course	[kɔːrs]	n. 高尔夫球场
block	[blɑːk]	n. 街区
extra	[ˈekstrə]	a. 额外的，补充的，附加的

Unit 4
Leisure Sports

charge	[tʃɑːrdʒ]	n.& v. 收费
equipment	[ɪˈkwɪpmənt]	n. 设备，装备；器材
golf club		高尔夫球棍；高尔夫俱乐部
all set		〈美俚〉准备就绪

Listen to a conversation about golf and answer the following questions.

1. Does Mark know how to play golf?
2. When will they play golf?
3. Is there any golf course nearby?
4. How much is it per person?

Task 2

Word Bank

hockey	[ˈhɒki]	n. 曲棍球；冰球
acre	[ˈeɪkə(r)]	n. 英亩

Listen to a news report about golf and fill in the blanks with the words you hear.

Golf is a game that is played with one ball and a set of metal sticks (called **1.**_____) that look somewhat like a weird version of **2.**_____ sticks. The entire game is played in a fairly large **3.**_____ ground that has no particular shape and is spread over an area as large as 100–200 **4.**_____. So, why do they need such a huge **5.**_____ to play this game when most other **6.**_____ games are played in much smaller fields? Also, while most outdoor ball games are played between two **7.**_____, golf is an individual game and each individual plays against his/her own strengths or **8.**_____.

Task 3

Listen to the five sentences from the recording, repeat each sentence after it is spoken, and then write it down.

1. _____.
2. _____.
3. _____.
4. _____.
5. _____.

Task 4

Discuss the following questions in your group.

1. What recreational sport do you like? Why?
2. Give a presentation on how to play golf.

Thank-you Letters

There are many reasons for writing a thank-you note. You may express your gratitude for the gift, for the help or support from a friend, for attendance at an important event, or for any other occasion where you feel it is necessary. A simple thank-you note shows your appreciation and credibility.

After the salutation in your letter, you should make clear the gift/service you received and express your appreciation for it. You'd better mention a specific detail about the gift/service, which will make your gratitude clearly felt by the recipient.

In the closing part, add a personal note to the recipient. It doesn't have to be very long or detailed, e.g. "I look forward to seeing you soon!"

What's more, avoid saying thank you too many times, and give some genuine statements. Restate your thank you in the last paragraphs. e.g. "Thanks again for the bike."

End the letter with a simple closing followed by your signature on the next line, e.g. "Love, (Line Break) Your Signature".

Unit 4
Leisure Sports

Sample

From

Ms. Bella Kerr

56 Thomas Avenues

Yellow Orchards

New Streets

California 6790

To

Ms. Lynda Filler

5/9 Queen's Apartment

56 Hollow Street

London 5768

Date: 8 July, 2014

Dear Lynda,

I am writing this to thank you for my lovely birthday gift. I got it exactly on the date of my birthday. The courier boy has delivered your gift just after you have called me to wish on birthday. Your best wishes were perfectly accompanied by your unique present.

Thank you so much for remembering my birthday and sending me the marvelous overcoat. It is of perfect fabric, size and color. Actually, it is the best I ever had. I will wear it on Christmas night. You are my darling friend who never forgets my birthday irrespective of the distance and the fast paced life.

You are a gift of God for me. You always share a special corner in my heart. True and caring friend like you is rare in this world. I can rely on you in my tough times as you have always held me in difficult moments. You are special and your choice of selecting gift is as special as you. I would like to invite you with your husband to celebrate this Christmas with us as we have not met since your wedding. Hope to see you soon.

With lots of love,

Bella

Follow-up Writing

You were invited to a golf tournament. You went there and had a nice day, enjoying the game and the party in which came many celebrities. As a big fan of golf, you had the most wonderful day. Write a thank-you letter to the organizer and express your appreciation.

Dear Sir or Madam,

_____

_____

_____

_____

Part One: Knowledge Preparation

As national intangible cultural heritage, originally used for worship and to pray for rain, Dragon Dance and Lion Dance are popular activities in the Chinese tradition. Lion Dance is often confused with Dragon Dance. The main difference between them is that a lion is normally operated by two dancers, while a dragon needs many people. Moreover, in a Lion Dance the performers' faces are only seen occasionally since they are inside the lion. In a Dragon Dance the performers' faces can be easily seen since the dragon is held on poles.

In recent centuries Dragon Dance and Lion Dance have spread all over the world with the Chinese immigrants settling in other countries. They are an indispensable part of most Chinese festivals and sometimes as part of special events. Over the past decade, in many parts of Southeast Asia, they have developed into international competitive sports. Modern Dragon Dance and Lion Dance have evolved from a general performance art into rich cultural and sports activities, with a combination of entertainment, festivities, multi-functional sports and fitness.

舞龙、舞狮是国家级非物质文化遗产，最初用于祭祀和祈雨，两者都是中国传统的大众活动。舞狮常与舞龙相混淆。它们之间的主要区别是，狮子通常由两个舞者表演，而龙则需要很多人。此外，舞狮时，只能偶尔看见表演者的面孔，因为他们藏在狮子里面。舞龙时，很容易看到表演者的面孔，因为人们将龙举在龙神棍上面。

近几个世纪以来，舞龙、舞狮随着中国移民在全球广为传播。它们是中国大多数节日不可缺少的一部分，有时也成为一些特殊活动的项目。过去十年里，在东南亚的许多地方，它们已经发展成为国际竞技体育。现代舞龙、舞狮已经从一般的表演艺术发展成为丰富多彩的文体活动，与娱乐、节庆、多功能体育和健身融为一体。

Unit 5
Dragon Dance and Lion Dance

Part Two   Reading

Text A

Dragon Dance
Lee Meiyu

1 The Dragon Dance, also known as *Longwu* or *Longdeng*, is a traditional Chinese sports activity as well as a dance performance involving a team of performers using poles to rhythmically move a dragon prop. The dance is performed during Chinese festive celebrations such as Lunar New Year, the Mid-Autumn Festival and some other special occasions.

Symbolism of the Dragon

2 The Dragon Dance is closely associated with the Chinese tradition of worshipping dragons. The dragon is considered to be one of the most auspicious creatures in Chinese culture. Chinese dragons are believed to have control over water, rain, hurricanes and floods. They also represent power, strength and good luck. The Chinese believe that performing the Dragon Dance during festivals and celebrations drives away evil spirits and ushers in good luck and blessings for the community.

Construction of the Dragon Prop

3 The dragon prop used for the dance varies in length, and typically ranges between 14 meters to 54 meters. It comprises three main segments: head, body and tail. The dragon's body is usually divided into sections of odd numbers of 9, 11 and 13, but can go up to as many as 29. By connecting these sections, the body of the dragon becomes flexible enough to twist and turn during a performance. The dragon head is commonly depicted with glaring eyes, an open jaw with a long, red pointed tongue, horns on its head and a white beard along the fringe of its chin.

4 The structure of the dragon prop is first formed using either bamboo or wood to shape it. This is followed by gluing either cloth or paper over the dragon's head, body and tail, connecting the separate parts to form the whole dragon. The prop is then painted, with the final, most important part of this process—the dotting of the dragon's eyes, which is believed to introduce the dragon's soul and is left in the hands of the most respected person in the community. Finally, bamboo poles are attached below the head, body and tail segments which the performers carry in order to animate the dragon.

Performance

5. Dragon Dance performers are usually martial artists or acrobats who are able to move their bodies rhythmically and synchronize their steps so that the dragon appears to move gracefully.

6. There are more than 20 basic stances in the dance, and a performer typically takes about half a year to master them and another one or two years before being ready to perform. Throughout the training, the performer has to build up strength and stamina with martial arts training in order to be strong enough to carry the dragon throughout the entire performance. Coordination between the dancers and the musicians is also a key to the performance, as the various movements of the dragon are marked by specific kinds of drum and gong rhythms.

7. When the performance starts, a man, holding a long pole with a dragon pearl affixed to the top, stands in front of the dragon's head. He swings the dragon pearl from side to side, while moving in tune to the sounds of the dragon drums and accompanying music. The dragon, held by its many bearers, chases the pearl and attempts to capture it, but is never successful. And so the dance continues, with the dragon pearl teasing the dragon and the dragon showing off its antics while trying to catch it. Sometimes, the performance includes two or three dragons all chasing the same dragon pearl. In this way, the Dragon Dance is widespread as a popular folk sports activity that is rich in Chinese culture.

Word Bank

rhythmically	['rɪðmɪkli]	adv. 有节奏地
prop	[prɑːp]	n. 道具；支柱，支撑物
auspicious	[ɔːˈspɪʃəs]	adj. 吉兆的，吉利的；幸运的
hurricane	[ˈhɜːrəkən]	n. 飓风，暴风
blessing	[ˈblesɪŋ]	n. 祝福，赐福；祷告
segment	[ˈsegmənt]	n. 段；部分
depict	[dɪˈpɪkt]	v. 描述；描画
fringe	[frɪndʒ]	n. 边缘
bamboo	[ˌbæmˈbuː]	n. 竹，竹子
glue	[gluː]	v. 黏合
animate	[ˈænɪmeɪt]	v. 使有生气；使活泼
acrobat	[ˈækrəbæt]	n. 杂技演员，特技演员
synchronize	[ˈsɪŋkrənaɪz]	v. 使……合拍；使……同步
stamina	[ˈstæmɪnə]	n. 毅力；精力；活力
coordination	[koʊˌɔːrdɪˈneɪʃn]	n. 协调，调和
affix	[əˈfɪks]	v. 贴上；署名

Unit 5
Dragon Dance and Lion Dance

swing	[swɪŋ]	v. 使旋转；挥舞；悬挂
tease	[tiːz]	v. 戏弄，挑逗；取笑
antics	['æntɪks]	n. 滑稽动作，古怪姿态

Phrases

as well as	也，又；既……又……；除……之外；此外
be associated with	和……联系在一起，与……有关
usher in	领进，引进
be divided into	被分成
odd numbers	单号
go up to	上升到
either... or...	二者择一的；要么……要么……
martial arts	武术；技击
show off	使突出；炫耀，卖弄

Proper Names

the Lunar New Year	农历新年
Mid-Autumn Festival	中秋节

Task 1 Text Organization

Read the text and fill in the blanks.

Paragraphs	Key Words	Supporting Details
Para. 1	Introduction of the Dragon Dance	• The Dragon Dance is a traditional Chinese sports activity as well as a _____, involving a team of performers using poles to rhythmically move a _____.
Paras. 2–4	Interpretation of the dragon	• Symbolism of the dragon: The Chinese believe that performing the Dragon Dance during festivals and celebrations drives away _____ and ushers in good luck and blessings for the community.

Paras. 2–4	Interpretation of the dragon	• Construction of the dragon prop: (1) 3 main segments: the head, _____ and _____. (2) 3 steps of making the dragon prop: First, it is formed using either _____ or wood to shape it. It is followed by _____ either cloth or paper over the whole dragon. Then, it is painted, with the final _____ of the dragon's eyes. Finally, bamboo poles are _____ below the dragon's three _____.
Paras. 5–7	Performance of the Dragon Dance	• Performers: (1) They are usually_____ or acrobats. (2) They are trained to _____ their strength, stamina and coordination. • Performance: (1) A man stands in front of the dragon's head and _____ the dragon pearl from side to side. (2) The dragon chases the pearl and attempts to _____ it, but is never successful. (3) The dance continues, with the dragon pearl _____ the dragon and the dragon showing off its antics.

Task 2 Reading Comprehension

Exercise 1

Read the text and decide whether the following statements are true (T) or false (F).

1. _____ The Dragon Dance is closely related to the Chinese tradition of showing devotion to dragons.
2. _____ The only material of the dragon is bamboo or wood.
3. _____ The most respectful person in the community is supposed to paint the dragon's eyes, which is believed to introduce the dragon's soul.
4. _____ Dragon Dance performers are usually acrobats or martial artists who are capable of moving their bodies in a flexible and graceful manner.

Unit 5
Dragon Dance and Lion Dance

5. _____ Sometimes, the performance includes two or three dragons chasing different dragon pearls.

Exercise 2

Read the text and answer the following questions.

1. When is the Dragon Dance performed?
2. Why do Chinese people like performing the Dragon Dance during festivals and celebrations?
3. What do you think about the appearance of a dragon prop?
4. How long will it take a performer to get ready for the Dragon Dance?
5. Is it easy for a dragon, held by its many bearers, to catch a dragon pearl? Why?

Task 3 Language in Use

Exercise 1

Match the underlined words in the left column with their corresponding meanings in the right column.

1. The Dragon Dance is a traditional Chinese dance performance involving a team of performers using poles to <u>rhythmically</u> move a dragon prop.	A. give lifelike qualities to
2. The dragon is considered to be one of the most <u>auspicious</u> creatures in Chinese culture.	B. in a manner that repeat a movement at regular intervals and form a regular pattern or beat
3. By connecting these sections, the body of the dragon becomes <u>flexible</u> enough to twist and turn during a performance.	C. the physical or mental energy needed to do a tiring activity for a long time
4. This is followed by <u>gluing</u> either cloth or paper over the dragon's head, body and tail, connecting the separate parts to form the whole dragon.	D. attached to
5. Finally, bamboo poles are attached below the head, body and tail segments, which the performers carry in order to <u>animate</u> the dragon.	E. be able to bend easily
6. Dragon Dance performers are usually martial artists or acrobats who are able to move their bodies rhythmically and <u>synchronize</u> their steps so that the dragon appears to move gracefully.	F. people whose employment involves carrying something

7. Throughout the training, the performer has to build up his or her strength and <u>stamina</u> with martial arts training in order to be strong enough to carry the dragon throughout the entire performance.

8. <u>Coordination</u> between the dancers and the musicians is also a key to the performance.

9. When the performance starts, a man, holding a long pole with a dragon pearl <u>affixed</u> to the top, stands in front of the dragon's head.

10. The dragon, held by its many <u>bearers</u>, chases the pearl and attempts to capture it, but is never successful.

G. indicating favorable circumstances and good luck

H. cause them to happen at the same time and speed as each other

I. joining things together, often for repairing broken things

J. the regulation of diverse elements into an integrated and harmonious operation

Exercise 2

Select one word for each blank from a list of choices given below and fill in the blank with its correct form.

| swing | mark | move | acrobat | blessing |
| antics | grace | master | strength | accompany |

Based on the Chinese tradition of worshipping dragons, Dragon Dance is usually performed to drive away evil spirits and usher in good luck and **1.**_____ during Chinese festive celebrations.

Performers are usually martial artists or **2.**_____. They are trained to rhythmically **3.**_____ their bodies and synchronize their steps in order to make the dragon dance in a flexible and **4.**_____ way. Typically, they take about half a year to **5.**_____ the skills and another one or two years to get ready for the performance, throughout which they are supposed to carry and animate the dragon. In addition to their **6.**_____ and stamina, their coordination with musicians is very important for the performance because specific kinds of drum and gong rhythms **7.**_____ different movements of the dragon.

When the performance starts, a man **8.**_____ a dragon pearl from side to side in order to make a fool of the dragon, held by its many bearers, with the rhythm of dragon drums and **9.**_____ music. Meanwhile, the dragon shows off its **10.**_____ while attempting to catch it unsuccessfully until the end of the Dragon Dance.

Exercise 3

Translate the following sentences into English.

1. 你大概不会想到把这么艰苦的劳动和快乐的事联系起来。(be associated with)
2. 有了这样的发展趋势，互联网时代将有可能迎来公民空前觉醒的时期。(usher)
3. 最初，武汉被划分为三个部分，即武昌、汉口和汉阳。(be divided into)
4. 在艺术作品中，他常被描绘成英俊的金发青年。(depict)
5. 他的邻居过去常常笑话他的破旧衣服。(tease)

Lion Dance

The Lion Dance is one of the most widespread folk dances and cultural sports in China. The lion is the king of animals. In Chinese tradition, the lion is regarded as a mascot, which can bring good luck. The dance has a long history with records of more than 2,000 years. During the Tang dynasty (618–907), the Lion Dance was already introduced into the royal family.

In the Lion Dance, two people act as a lion; one waving the lion head and the other waving the lion body and tail; or one performer acts as a cub, another person is needed to hold a silk ball to play with the lion.

Skill is the most important thing while performing the Lion Dance. After long years of development, there are various lion dances. It's one of the most popular programs of dance and acrobatics troupes today.

When it is the Lantern Festival or any of other festive occasions, people often organize the Lion Dance. If well performed, the Lion Dance is believed to bring luck and happiness.

Types by Style

The performance is divided into *Wenshi* (civil lion) and *Wushi* (martial lion) according to the performing styles. *Wenshi* depicts the images of a lion, which is docile and funny. It scratches, licks or dozes off. In some areas, the lion player wears a mask. For instance, there are the Luohan (Arhat) Playing with Lion in Sichuan and Hunan provinces and the Laughing Monk Playing with Lion in Shanxi Province.

Wushi portrays the power of the lion. Besides the usual jumping, falling and tumbling, performers will also show their excellent techniques by climbing upon a high table or by stepping on five wooden stakes. For instance, the Gaotai (High Terrace) Lion Dance of Sichuan Province has to be performed on seven high tables, which makes the performance very difficult. In recent years, the Lion Dance in Beijing combined the advantages of other types to become a new style.

Types by Geography

Based on geographical features, the Lion Dance has developed into two major genres—the Northern Lion Dance and the Southern Lion Dance.

The Northern Lion Dance has a longer history than any other forms of Lion Dance. It is said that in the Northern Wei dynasty (386–534), Emperor Wudi launched an expedition to Hexi in Gansu Province, and took captive of more than 100,000 Mongols. The emperor ordered the Mongols to perform dance and other entertainment. More than 30 Mongolian warriors held wood carved animal heads, two big and five small, and wore animal skins, dancing before the emperor. The emperor was very pleased and named it Northern Wei Auspicious Lion, and allowed the captives to return home. Subsequently, the Lion Dance became popular in northern China, and the Northern Lion Dance came into being.

The Northern Lion Dance mainly focuses on the performance of the martial Lion Dance, i.e. the Auspicious Lion of the Northern Wei dynasty. Guided by the lion dancers, the lion writhes, falls forward, jumps and makes a bow, as well as some other highly difficult movements such as walking on wooden or bamboo stakes, jumping over a table, and stepping on a rolling ball, etc.

The Southern Lion Dance mainly focuses on the performance of the civilized Lion Dance. The performance attaches much attention to the movements like scratching an itch, shaking the hair, licking the hair and so on.

As can be seen from the above classification, no matter what type of the Lion Dance is performed, the movements are rooted in the traditional Chinese martial arts, also known as Wushu. Gradually, the Lion Dance has gained popularity across the globe and has now grown into an internationally competitive sport.

Word Bank

mascot	['mæskɔːt]	n. 吉祥物；福神（亦作 mascotte）
royal	['rɔɪəl]	adj. 皇家的
cub	[kʌb]	n. 幼兽
troupe	[truːp]	n. 剧团
docile	['dɑːsl]	adj. 温顺的，驯服的
scratch	[skrætʃ]	v. 抓，搔
mask	[mæsk]	n. 面具
portray	[pɔːr'treɪ]	v. 描绘；扮演
tumble	['tʌmbl]	v. 摔倒；滚动；打滚
stake	[steɪk]	n. 桩，棍子
terrace	['terəs]	n. 平台；梯田；阳台

Unit 5
Dragon Dance and Lion Dance

launch	[lɔːntʃ]	v.	发起，发动
entertainment	[ˌentər'teɪnmənt]	n.	娱乐，消遣；款待
warrior	['wɔːriər]	n.	战士，勇士
subsequently	['sʌbsɪkwəntli]	adv.	随后，其后；后来
writhe	[raɪð]	v.	翻滚；蠕动
itch	[ɪtʃ]	n.	痒

Phrases

folk dances	民间舞蹈
according to	根据
doze off	打瞌睡，打盹，困倦
take captive	活捉，俘虏
attach attention to	重视

Proper Names

the Luohan (Arhat) Playing with Lion	罗汉戏狮
the Laughing Monk Playing with Lion	笑和尚耍狮
the Gaotai (High Terrace) Lion Dance	高台舞狮
Northern Wei Auspicious Lion	北魏瑞狮

Critical Reading and Thinking

Read the text and decide whether the following statements are true (T) or false (F).

1. _____ The Lion Dance is one of the most widespread urban dances in China.

2. _____ In the Lion Dance, two people act as a lion, and another person is supposed to hold a silk ball to play with the lion.

3. _____ Nowadays, there are various lion dances, which have become very popular programs of dance and acrobatics organizations.

4. _____ People often organize a Lion Dance in Mid-Autumn Festivals and other festive occasions.

5. _____ The performance is divided into *Wenshi* (civil lion) and *Wushi* (martial lion) according to the geographical styles.

6. _____ It is very difficult to perform the Gaotai (High Terrace) Lion Dance on seven high tables.

7. _____ Based on performing features, the Lion Dance has developed into two major genres—the Northern Lion Dance and the Southern Lion Dance.

8. _____ The Southern Lion Dance has a longer history than any other forms of Lion Dance.

9. _____ The performance of the Northern Lion Dance is primarily associated with the martial arts.

10. _____ The Southern Lion Dance is principally characterized by gentle and comic performance.

Translation

Translate the following sentences into Chinese.

1. In Chinese tradition, the lion is regarded as a mascot, which can bring good luck.
2. In the Lion Dance, two people act as a lion; one waving the lion head and the other waving the lion body and tail; or one performer acts as a cub, another person is needed to hold a silk ball to play with the lion.
3. *Wushi* portrays the power of the lion. Besides the usual jumping, falling and tumbling, performers will also show their excellent techniques by climbing upon a high table or by stepping on five wooden stakes.
4. Subsequently, the Lion Dance became popular in northern China, and the Northern Lion Dance came into being.
5. The performance attaches much attention to the movements like scratching an itch, shaking the hair, licking the hair and so on.

Part Three — Listening and Speaking

Task 1

Word Bank

evil	[ˈiːvl]	*adj.* 邪恶的
concept	[ˈkɑːnsept]	*n.* 观念，概念
man-eating	[ˈmæn iːtɪŋ]	*adj.* 吃人的；食人的

Unit 5
Dragon Dance and Lion Dance

monster	[ˈmɑːnstər]	n. 怪物；巨人
symbolize	[ˈsɪmbəlaɪz]	v. 象征
dignity	[ˈdɪgnəti]	n. 尊严；高贵
wisdom	[ˈwɪzdəm]	n. 智慧，才智
protector	[prəˈtektər]	n. 保护者
guardian	[ˈgɑːrdiən]	n. 保护人，守护者
acrobatic	[ˌækrəˈbætɪk]	adj. 杂技的；特技的

Listen to a conversation between a Chinese student and a foreign student talking about the Chinese Dragon Dance and Lion Dance and answer the following questions.

1. When are the Dragon Dance and Lion Dance performed?
2. What is the purpose of the dances?
3. What is the dragon like in the Western concept?
4. What does the dragon symbolize in Chinese culture?
5. What's the lion considered to be by Chinese people?

##

Word Bank

firework	[ˈfaɪərwɜːrk]	n. 烟火
decade	[ˈdekeɪd]	n. 十年
artistry	[ˈɑːrtɪstri]	n. 艺术性
playacting	[ˈpleɪˈæktɪŋ]	n. 演戏；假装

Listen to a news report from CNN and choose the best answer to each question.

1. What's the most recognized celebration of the Lunar New Year around the world?
   - **A.** Setting off fireworks.
   - **B.** Eating dumplings.
   - **C.** The Lion Dance.
   - **D.** Giving money in red envelops.

2. How many lion dancers has master Andy Kwok instructed over the last two decades?
   - **A.** 8.
   - **B.** 14.
   - **C.** 40.
   - **D.** 500.

3. Beyond the Lunar New Year, what does the team do?
   - **A.** It competes in various competitions in Asia.
   - **B.** It performs at business openings.
   - **C.** It performs at weddings.
   - **D.** All of the above.

4. What's the Lion Dance based on?

   A. Kung fu techniques.   B. Artistry.

   C. Playacting.   D. Dancing.

Task 3

Listen to the five sentences from the recording, repeat each sentence after it is spoken, and then write it down.

1. _____.
2. _____.
3. _____.
4. _____.
5. _____.

Task 4

Discuss the following questions in your group.

1. Have you ever seen a Dragon Dance or Lion Dance?
2. Would you like to join a Dragon Dance or Lion Dance team? Why or why not?
3. Why are dragons important in Chinese culture?
4. What can be done to promote the development of the Dragon Dance and Lion Dance?

Part Four Writing

Congratulation Letters

A congratulation letter is used for praising a person or a team on their success. This letter is a great gesture to maintain personal as well as professional relationships. Through this letter, you can talk about the exemplary qualities that helped a person to achieve his/her goals in life. Such a letter makes the recipient proud of his/her success.

You need to congratulate a person in the very beginning of the letter. The letter should start off on a joyful note. You have to be prompt in sending congratulatory message. Draft the letter as soon as you get the good news and dispatch it to the person who has succeeded.

You should mention how these achievements are significant. The letter should be full of enthusiasm and happiness, while at the same time, direct and simple. The tone must be soft and positive. Be honest in expressing your thoughts. Don't be pompous.

Make sure that the letter is as brief as possible. You should limit it to one pager.

Sample

August 15th, 2011

My Dear Friend Daniel,

It gives me immense pleasure to know that you won the first prize in the essay writing competition organized at the University College. Hearty congratulations! I read all the details of the competition in the newspaper yesterday and I must say, yours is a splendid achievement. Winning a first prize among the hundred odd entries is no child's play. I am proud of you Daniel. I am proud to have such a friend.

Daniel, I have seen your growth as a writer. You love writing; I know and I have seen the efforts you have taken to groom yourself as a writer. You read a lot. You try to remember a lot and I think these are some of your qualities which help you win competitions. I am sure, you will bloom as a prolific writer in the coming future. I wish you all luck for your future achievements. Congratulations once again!

Your friend,

Emily

Follow-up Writing

Suppose you are a member of the judge commission. You are writing a congratulation letter to a dragon and lion dance team who has recently won an award in the National Dragon and Lion Dance Competition.

You should point out the ranking as well as the reason for the judge commission to decide on the victory. You can use the following information on the next page.

368 Youyi Street
Hubei University, Wuhan
June 24, 2016

The Judge Commission of National Dragon and Lion Dance Competition
842 Chang'an Street
Beijing, China

Dear …

_____

_____

_____

_____

Unit 6
Sports Culture

Part One — Knowledge Preparation

American football is the most popular sport in the United States, and is ranked the top out of four professional sports in North America. Since the 1960s, American football have surpassed basketball and baseball becoming the most favored sport in America. In every January and February, two winners from American Football Conference (AFC) and National Football Conference (NFC) will compete for Vince Lombardi Trophy in a preassigned city. The final championship is called the Super Bowl, occupying more than half of the audience rating in American and over 150 countries' TV relay on the competition worldwide. Super Bowl Sunday has been an annual festivity. Although it is not an official holiday, Super Bowl Sunday is the top-rated sport TV program in America.

美式橄榄球是美国最流行的运动，为北美四大职业体育之首。自20世纪60年代，美式橄榄球已经超越篮球和棒球成为美国最受喜爱的运动项目。每年的一二月，AFC（美国橄榄球联会）和NFC（国家橄榄球联会）的两个联会冠军会在某个指定的城市争夺文斯·隆巴迪奖杯，这个总冠军赛也就是"超级碗"，拥有超过一半美国家庭的电视收视率，同时全世界有超过150个国家电视转播这场比赛。"超级碗星期天"已经成为年度大戏，基本上成为一个非官方假日，该赛事同时也是全美收视率最高的体育电视节目。

Part Two — Reading

Text A

Why Football Is Essential to American Culture

1 Let me start off by saying that, when I was growing up, my family couldn't have cared less about football. As an American household, we fought the norm (or at least my parents did) and refused to dive into the culture. This was weird because not only did my mother work directly with Paul Allen, but my father played football for over half of his life. It wasn't until I hit high school that I began to really notice that football was important to the social aspect of American culture.

2 It was freshman year, and it was raining. Hard. I was standing in the metal bleachers, clad in a ridiculously colorful sweatshirt matching those of the players on the field and trying not to slowly freeze while standing around each other yelling at the opposing team. This to me, seemed to be the most ridiculous thing on the planet.

3 I couldn't understand how people put so much value into a sport that they didn't even play. Why did it matter who won or lost? Why was it so important? Why did people care?

4 The Mondays following every football game were always filled with recaps—either over the loud speakers at the school or from the players themselves. And the Friday's before the games were dedicated to the players as they waltzed around school donning their jerseys and khakis. It all seemed too stupid.

5 It was my senior year, and I was bored. Almost off to college and almost done with high school forever. I had nothing to focus my time on. When one of my friends offered me a position as a football manager for the high school team, I figured, why not? I have nothing else to do. So every day I'd go to practice and handle the water, fill the bottles, help with ice and injuries, and make sure that everyone had their gear. During games, I'd do the same.

6 I began to notice that there were a lot of legacies on the team: boys whose fathers, grandfathers, and maybe even great-grandfathers had played. Sometimes the parents would come to watch their sons practice and they would get a gleam in their eyes, their faces filling with pride and joy. I began to realize that football helped bring families together; it was something so universal that sons, grandsons, and great-grandsons could all participate in it.

7 When I stood on the field, amidst the startlingly bright lights and sweaty players, I would find myself looking back at the audience, trying to see what they saw. I would look back and see fervent fans rallying up the crowd, trying to get them to be so loud that the players could hear their support on the field during an important play.

8 When the team won, I noticed that everyone acted like the town had achieved a great victory. Like we had all won a war. It was then that I realized that people had, in a sense, won a war; they waited their whole week, through laborious jobs and hard family struggles, to see their team triumph and stand by them when they did. The crowd had won the game just as much as the players had.

9 When the team lost, it was like everyone had lost the lottery. Sometimes I saw tears from fans when the loss was particularly hard to swallow. We had lost a battle. We had lost a war.

10 When I moved on to college, my football family grew exponentially to include thousands upon thousands of fans. It was like the small community I had grown up in back home exploded into a teeming mass of crimson and gold. We fought with our team, we won with our team, and we lost with our team. We were a family because of our team. We were wearing the same colors, yelling the same chants as our parents and grandparents had.

⑪ Football allows its fans to become passionate and supportive. The rules of football are—while disputable sometimes—universal. Whether you are a custodian or a CEO, an actress or a librarian, a student or an adult; the rules of football remain the same. Because of this, everyone can understand them. It allows us to engage in debate and discussion. It encourages learning and active participation in an event that everyone can see and interpret, listen and watch, appreciate and love.

⑫ Football connects us, as a nation, under the common goal of seeing our teams win. We can support whoever we want for whatever reason we choose, we can debate and bicker with fellow fans or frenemies from other teams, and we can share a love of something universal, global, and magical.

⑬ Football is essential to American culture because it makes us a family. It brings us together, it allows us to share in something greater than ourselves, it gives us a reason not to hate Sundays, Mondays and Thursdays, and it gives us the opportunity to fall in love with something spectacular.

Word Bank

essential	[ɪˈsenʃl]	adj. 基本的；必要的；本质的
household	[ˈhaʊshoʊld]	n. 家庭；同住一所房子的人
norm	[nɔːrm]	n. 标准，规范
bleacher	[ˈbliːtʃər]	n.（运动场的）露天看台，露天座位
ridiculously	[rɪˈdɪkjələsli]	adv. 可笑地，荒谬地
freeze	[friːz]	v. 冻结，冷冻；僵硬
recap	[ˈriːkæp]	n. 扼要重述
waltz	[wɔːls]	v. 跳华尔兹舞；旋转；轻快地走
don	[dɑːn]	v. 穿上（衣服）
jersey	[ˈdʒɜːrzi]	n. 运动衫，毛线衫
khaki	[ˈkɑːki]	n. 卡其裤；卡其服装
gear	[gɪr]	n.（用于特定活动的）设备；服装
gleam	[gliːm]	n. 微光；闪光；瞬息的一现
amidst	[əˈmɪd]	prep. 在……当中
startlingly	[ˈstɑːrtlɪŋli]	adv. 惊人地，使人惊奇地
fervent	[ˈfɜːrvənt]	adj. 强烈的；炽热的；热心的
laborious	[ləˈbɔːriəs]	adj. 勤劳的；艰苦的；费劲的
triumph	[ˈtraɪʌmf]	n. 胜利，凯旋；欢欣
lottery	[ˈlɑːtəri]	n. 彩票；碰运气的事
swallow	[ˈswɑːloʊ]	v. 完全相信；忍受；吞下

Unit 6
Sports Culture

exponentially	[ˌekspə'nenʃəli]	adv. 迅速增长地，迅猛发展地
teeming	['tiːmɪŋ]	adj. 多产的，丰富的；热闹的
chant	[tʃænt]	n. 圣歌，赞美诗；吟唱
passionate	['pæʃənət]	adj. 热情的；热烈的，激昂的
disputable	[dɪ'spjuːtəbl]	adj. 可争议的
custodian	[kʌ'stoʊdiən]	n. 管理人；监护人；保管人
frenemy	['frenəmi]	n. 亦敌亦友
spectacular	[spek'tækjələr]	adj. 壮观的，惊人的

Phrases

start off	出发，开始
dive into	钻研，探究，探索
yell at	对……喊
dedicate to	把（时间、精力等）用于
explode into	爆发出……
a mass of	大量的
engage in	从事（参加）
bicker with	与……拌嘴

Task 1 Text Organization

Read the text and fill in the blanks.

Paragraphs	Key Words	Supporting Details
Para. 1	Football is important to _____.	• When I was growing up, my family couldn't _____. • My mother worked with Paul Allen, my father _____.
Paras. 2–4	My _____ about football	• _____ seemed to be the most ridiculous thing on the planet. • I couldn't understand _____. • _____ seemed too stupid.

87

Paras. 5–10	My _____ about football	• I was offered a position as _____ for the high school team. • I began to realize that _____. • When I stood on the field, I would find myself _____, trying to _____. • When I moved on to college, my football family _____ _____.
Paras. 11–13	Football is _____ to American culture.	• Football allows everyone to engage in, whether you are __ _____. • Football connects people who have the common goal of _____ and share _____. • Football makes us a _____ and gives us the chance _____.

Task 2 Reading Comprehension

Exercise 1

Read the text and decide whether the following statements are true (T) or false (F).

1. _____ When I was growing up, my family didn't care about football.
2. _____ I began to really notice that football was important to the social aspect of American culture when I was at high school.
3. _____ When I was a freshman, I couldn't understand why so many people put their energies on football.
4. _____ It was so usual that parents who played football didn't want their children to take part in this sport.
5. _____ When football teams lost game, their fans would feel very disappointed and wouldn't support them anymore.

Exercise 2

Read the text and answer the following questions.

1. What did the author's parents think about football when he was a child?
2. What was the author's job when he was offered a position as a manager in a football team?
3. What did the author notice about a lot of legacies on the football teams?

Unit 6
Sports Culture

4. Why can everyone understand the rules of football according to the author?
5. Why is football essential to American culture?

Task 3 Language in Use

Exercise 1

Match the underlined words in the left column with their corresponding meanings in the right column.

1. As an American household, we fought the <u>norm</u> and refused to dive into the culture.

    A. extremely important or absolutely necessary to a particular subject, situation, or activity

2. It gives us the opportunity to fall in love with something <u>spectacular</u>.

    B. religious songs or prayers that are sung on only a few notes

3. Football is <u>essential</u> to American culture because it makes us a family.

    C. very rapidly

4. The rules of football are—while <u>disputable</u> sometimes— universal.

    D. very foolish

5. We were wearing the same colors, yelling the same <u>chants</u> as our parents and grandparents had.

    E. traditions that pass on from generation to generation

6. When I moved on to college, my football family grew <u>exponentially</u> to include thousands upon thousands of fans.

    F. way of behaving that is considered normal in a particular society

7. I would look back and see <u>fervent</u> fans rallying up the crowd.

    G. relating to everyone in the world or everyone in a particular group or society

8. I began to notice that there were a lot of <u>legacies</u> on the team.

    H. capable of being argued

9. It was something so <u>universal</u> that sons, grandsons, and great-grandsons could all participate in it.

    I. showing strong feelings and be very enthusiastic about something

10. This is seemed to be the most <u>ridiculous</u> thing on the planet.

    J. very impressive or dramatic

Exercise 2

Select one word for each blank from a list of choices given below and fill the blank with its correct form.

| defend | score | invade | artificial | accumulate |
| ultimate | territory | unique | cover | battle |

American football is a 1._____ sport. It is a game about gaining 2._____ as much as it is about 3._____ points. When two teams step onto a football field, each is 4._____ for every inch it can take from the other. Each team wants to 5._____ the field that is behind it and 6._____ the field in front of it. 7._____, they want to gain enough ground to score a touchdown or field goal. Football is a game of inches played on a field measured in yards. English measurements are used to track movements on the field. Teams succeed based on how many yards they 8._____ or allow. An official football field is a rectangle that is 120 yards (110 m) long and 53 yards (49 m) wide. Most fields are 9._____ in grass and set in an outdoor stadium. Some fields are made of 10._____ turf, which you'll find in many of the indoor stadiums.

Exercise 3

Translate the following sentences into English.
1. 她一直在钻研美国文学。(dive into)
2. 接力赛跑的基本要点是讲究团队合作。(essential)
3. 如果温度降到零摄氏度以下，水就会结冰。(freeze)
4. 它们是我们文学产业中的瑰宝，是我们共同的遗产。(legacy)
5. 你应该多参加一些你喜欢的体育运动。(engage in)

How the Internet Is Shaping Swim Culture

If you are currently reading this article, you are the prime example of our Internet-driven era. Most likely, you are on your phone, computer, or other personal device. The way we read both informative and entertainment articles has changed drastically just within the last four years, thanks to the ever-developing age of the Internet. The culture of the sport of swimming has also changed, ushered in by a technologically inclined generation.

There are various components of the Internet as a whole. Within social media, an important part of the Internet, a shared bond is created that connects each and every person as an audience.

For the swimming community, aquatic-related businesses bring together an even larger swimming audience, as they entertain, share media, and market themselves toward their followers. Today, some of the biggest names in the media business of our beloved sport sit down to discuss the benefits of swimming in media.

Zach Kent is the owner of the Twitter handle @iSwimWithIssues, which currently caters to 104,100 followers. This number has grown over the course of three years after Kent decided to create the social media account out of boredom on the way home from a championship meet. He has other platforms such as Instagram, Facebook and a website that features swim apparel, all of which target club and high school-aged swimmers.

"Social media allows swimmers to come together and appreciate common ideas," Kent said. "Much of these ideas, tweets, posts or thoughts are such that they'll resonate through the entire swim community. This allows for swimmers to share and laugh about and appreciate the sport of swimming."

Essentially, that is what Kent is doing, hand-in-hand with the Internet: creating a tighter-knit family.

This makes it easy to bring what swimmers want, as an audience, to the table.

"Swimming is a world of its own," Kent said. "If you're a swimmer yourself, you'll fit in perfectly fine and know exactly how to relate to other swimmers."

Being a swimmer himself makes it easier to market to his followers.

"I know firsthand that swimmers like to show off that they swim. So, I thought, why shouldn't our apparel do just that?" From there, the success of iSwimWithIssues reached new heights, and continues to do so.

Then there is Michael Plantamura, a rising college freshman and the owner of a network of 350,000 followers combined from Facebook, Instagram, and Snapchat, all of which branched out from the Twitter handle @Swimmin101. Additionally, he is a co-owner of the subscription box Swimfluence, which has been recently featured on USA Swimming.

Plantamura agrees with the fact that the many forms of social media are a positive factor for the swimming culture.

"People get on and see how amazing the sport of swimming is and see the bond that all swimmers share, and how it has a community unlike any other sport. Through social media we are able to strengthen that bond between swimmers and help people connect."

Plantamura also seized the opportunity to market the sport to its beloved athletes. His Internet-based network sells many different kinds of swimming-related merchandise. Likewise, the Swimfluence idea was born out of a desire to improve a swimmer's life in and out of the pool with special surprise items.

Yet despite his accomplishments, Plantamura humbly admits that he never imagined his Twitter account would come as far as it has over the past two years.

"I was just another swimmer that wanted to share all of the funny thoughts that had gone through my head during practice. And it just happened that a lot of other people liked what I was tweeting."

Simply put, the best kind of person to relate to when you're a swimmer is another swimmer.

Word Bank

inclined	[ɪnˈklaɪnd]	adj. 趋向于……的
bond	[bɑːnd]	n. 密切联系
aquatic	[əˈkwætɪk]	adj. 水生的；水栖的；在水中或水面进行的 n. 水上运动；水生植物或动物
market	[ˈmɑːrkɪt]	v. 在市场上出售；做买卖
boredom	[ˈbɔːrdəm]	n. 厌倦；令人厌烦的事物
platform	[ˈplætfɔːrm]	n. 平台
apparel	[əˈpærəl]	n. 服装；衣服
target	[ˈtɑːrgɪt]	v. 把……作为目标；规定……的指标
resonate	[ˈrezəneɪt]	v. 共鸣；共振
hand-in-hand	[ˈhændɪnˈhænd]	adj. 并进的；手拉手的；亲密的
firsthand	[ˌfɜːrstˈhænd]	adv.（来源、资料等）第一手地，直接地
subscription	[səbˈskrɪpʃn]	n.（电视或频道）付费
strengthen	[ˈstreŋθn]	v. 加强，巩固
beloved	[bɪˈlʌvd]	adj. 心爱的；挚爱的
merchandise	[ˈmɜːrtʃəndaɪs]	n. 商品；货物
accomplishment	[əˈkɑːmplɪʃmənt]	n. 成就；完成；技艺，技能
humbly	[ˈhʌmbli]	adv. 谦逊地

Phrases

sit down to a discussion	进行讨论
cater to	设法适应（……的需要）；迎合（……的爱好）
fit in	适应，适合
get on	使开始，进展
seize the opportunity	抓住机遇，抓住机会
relate to	涉及，有关
simply put	简言之，简单地说

Unit 6
Sports Culture

Proper Names

Twitter	推特（社交网站）
Instagram	一款图片分享应用
Facebook	脸书（社交网站）
Snapchat	色拉布，一款由斯坦福大学两位学生开发的"阅后即焚"的照片分享应用。利用该应用程序，用户可以拍照、录制视频、添加文字和图画，并将它们发送给自己在该应用上的好友。这些照片及视频被称为"快照"（Snaps），而该软件的用户自称为"快照族"（Snubs）。

Critical Reading and Thinking

Read the text and decide whether the following statements are true (T) or false (F).

1. _____ The culture of the sport of swimming has changed due to the fast development of Internet.
2. _____ Aquatic-related businesses get a lot of benefits from social media.
3. _____ This number of Zach Kent's Twitter followers has dropped after he decided to create another social media account.
4. _____ Kent said that it was difficult to use social media to do business about swimming.
5. _____ Plantamura agrees with the fact that the many forms of social media made a positive impact on the swimming culture.
6. _____ Social media helps build the connection between swimmers and audiences.
7. _____ Plantamura only sells swimsuit through his social media account.
8. _____ Plantamura's Swimfluence ideas contribute a lot to improving swimmer's life.
9. _____ Plantamura has predicted that his Twitter account would make profits as far as it has over the past two years.
10. _____ As a swimmer, Plantamura is very pleased to share all of the funny thoughts during practice with other swimmers through Twitter.

Translation

Translate the following sentences into Chinese.

1. The way we read both informative and entertainment articles has changed drastically just within the last four years, thanks to the ever-developing age of the Internet.
2. The culture of the sport of swimming has changed, ushered in by a technologically inclined generation.

3. Within social media, a shared bond is created that connects each and every person as an audience.

4. Today, some of the biggest names in the media business of our beloved sport sit down to discuss the benefits of swimming in media.

5. People get on and see how amazing the sport of swimming is and see the bond that all swimmers share, and how it has a community unlike any other sport.

Part Three Listening and Speaking

Task 1

Word Bank

rectangular	[rek'tæŋgjələr]	adj. 矩形的
goalpost	['goʊlpoʊst]	n. 球门柱；门柱
oval-shaped	['əʊvlʃeɪpt]	adj. 椭圆形的
touchdown	['tʌtʃdaʊn]	n. 触地得分

Listen to a conversation about American football and answer the following questions.

1. How many players are on the field in an American football game?
2. What do they play with?
3. What does the defense team do?
4. What does Tod think is the best thing about the sport?
5. Why are players required to wear football helmet and shoulder pads?

Task 2

Word Bank

predict	[prɪ'dɪkt]	v. 预报，预言
commercial	[kə'mɜːrʃl]	n. 商业广告 adj. 商业的；营利的
halftime	[ˌhæf 'taɪm]	n. 中场休息

Unit 6
Sports Culture

Massachusetts	马萨诸塞州（美国）
Georgia	乔治亚州（美国）
the Super Bowl	超级碗（美国国家足球联盟年度冠军赛）
National Football League	美国国家足球联盟
Atlanta Falcons	亚特兰大猎鹰队（职业美式足球球队）
New England Patriots	新英格兰爱国者队（职业美式足球球队）

Listen to a news report and complete the following sentences with the information you hear.

1. The Patriots will try to win _____ Super Bowl title; the Falcons are aiming to win _____.
2. In a public opinion study, _____ of those questioned said they thought the Atlanta Falcons would win. It seems that many fans might be _____ the Patriots win the Super Bowl.
3. Even people who do not pay any attention to football during _____ watch the Super Bowl. Last year, almost _____ people watched the game on television.
4. Some people are more interested in _____ that play during the broadcast. Many are also interested in _____.
5. Some popular food items include pizza, _____, chips, and, of course, _____.

Task 3

Listen to the five sentences from the recording, repeat each sentence after it is spoken, and then write it down.

1. _____.
2. _____.
3. _____.
4. _____.
5. _____.

Task 4

Discuss the following questions in your group.

1. What's the difference between American football and European football?
2. Why is football essential to the Americans?
3. What's the most popular sport in China?
4. How is American sports culture different from that in China?

Résumés

A résumé is a document used by a person to present his/her backgrounds and skills to secure a new employment. A typical résumé contains a "summary" of relevant job experience and education. In many contexts, a résumé is typically limited to one or two pages of size A4 or letter-size, highlighting only those experiences and qualifications that the applicant considers most relevant to the desired position. Résumés can vary in style and length, but should always contain accurate contact information of the job seeker.

Sample

Brian Christoff
123 Fogbound Street • Portland, ME 12345 • (123) 555-1234 • behristoff@unknown.com

JOB OBJECTIVE
A position in Marketing/Sales with L.L. Bean sporting goods

QUALIFICATIONS
- Three years as member of a sales team with a substantial retail client base.
- Natural ability to promote products and build rapport through listening and communication skills.

PROFESSIONAL HISTORY
2010-present Member of Sales Team that worked for:
Smith Barncy, Portland, 2013-present
PaineWebber, Portland, 2011-2013
Alex Brown, Portland, 2010-2011

- Achieved highest bonus level for exceptional performance on sales team with a targeted client base of retail and institutional accounts.
- Promoted within this team headed by three financial consultants who worked for two major investment firms and went on to form their own company under the Smith Barney umbrella.
- Generated sales through weekly phone calls to account base of 150 clients.
- Commended for building strong rapport with clients by understanding their needs and clearly explaining products.
- Created "syndicate calendars," marketing pieces used by the sales, trading, and research departments.
- Served as liaison between parties to coordinate schedules, payments, and allocations.

2007-2009   Waitperson   Bart and Yeti's Restaurant, Vail, CO

EDUCATION
B.A., Psychology, Fort Lewis College, Durango, CO, 2006

ADVENTURE/SPORTS
- Completed a two-month solo trip throughout Central and Eastern Europe.
- Actively participate in sports: Triathlons   Hiking   Running
                                    Downhill skiing   Cycling   Camping
                                    Back country skiing Swimming

Unit 6
Sports Culture

Follow-up Writing

Write a résumé for your job seeking. You can include basic information such as address, education, awards or qualifications, job experiences, skills and so on.

Unit 7
Sports Science

Part One — Knowledge Preparation

With the growing popularity of youth team sports such as soccer and basketball, there has been a substantial increase in the number of athletic injuries among adolescents. Each year, many high school students experience season-ending or even career-ending athletic injuries, yet surprisingly little is known about how to avoid these injuries or rehabilitate youth after such an injury.

Currently, the best advice for adolescent athletes is to warm up and condition appropriately before beginning a competitive season, and for coaches and parents to be aware of the risk factors for injury, which include movement and coordination differences between the legs, muscle weakness and poor conditioning leading to early fatigue. Adolescent athletes should be encouraged to participate in a variety of sports in order to develop coordination and strength throughout the body and avoid early specialization into a single sport that could lead to muscle strength imbalances and, potentially, increase the risk of injury.

随着青少年足球和篮球等团体运动的日益普及，青少年运动员的运动损伤的数量显著增加。每年，许多高中生都会因为扭伤经历赛季，甚至是职业生涯的终结，但却很少有人知道如何避免受伤或是如何进行伤后恢复。

目前，对青少年运动员的最佳建议是在赛季前热身，并提醒教练和家长们要注意危险因素造成的伤害，其中包括运动和双腿的协调，肌肉无力和不良调节导致早期疲劳。应该鼓励青少年运动员参加各种不同的运动项目来锻炼全身的协调性和肌肉力度，尽量避免对某一项运动的过早专业化训练，否则会导致肌肉发展的不均衡，还会增加潜在的受伤风险。

Unit 7
Sports Science

Part Two — Reading

Are Children Drinking Enough During Exercise?
David A. White, PhD., CEP

1 By some estimates, two-thirds of child athletes are dehydrated during exercise. Proper hydration is vital for regulating temperature, maintaining blood volume and eliminating waste. Water loss from sweat, urine and increased metabolism can lead to dehydration in active youth, with potentially serious consequences.

2 One of the primary reasons for children to hydrate properly is to maintain an appropriate temperature. While adult bodies are cooled mostly through evaporation of sweat, children's bodies cool mostly through "dry" conduction and convection. For example, when a child's body temperature increases while exercising or being in a warm environment, the blood vessels near the surface of the skin enlarge. The body sends warm blood to the dilated blood vessels to release heat to the surface of the skin, similar to the way a radiator works in a car. The cooled blood then returns to the center of the body. A dehydrated child, however, does not have enough blood available to be transported to the skin and the exercising muscle at the same time. As a result, children have a higher risk of heat-related illnesses, such as muscle cramps, heat exhaustion or heat stroke. Dehydrated children also risk a drop in blood pressure, which can make them feel dizzy or light headed during or immediately after a bout of exercise, with the potential for injury.

3 In addition to affecting thermoregulation, dehydration in children can have particularly strong effects on both exercise ability and performance of mental and physical tasks. In adults, a loss of two percent of body weight from dehydration can cause considerable decreases in the ability to perform these tasks. However, in prepubescent children, these changes are evident at a loss of only one percent of body weight, leading to possible loss of coordination, decreased energy and muscle fatigue.

4 The easiest way to determine dehydration in a child is to monitor the color of the child's urine. Another method is to weigh the child before and after the activity. A general rule of thumb is the urine should be similar to lightly colored lemonade. Body weight decreases of one to three percent represent minimal dehydration. Decreases of three to five percent represent significant

dehydration, and more than five percent represent serious dehydration. Be aware: the sensation of thirst is not a reliable marker of adequate hydration.

5 What should active children drink? Non-caffeinated and non-carbonated fluids are best throughout the day and during and after physical activity. Children should rehydrate slowly, but steadily, within two hours of exercising, preferably with water. Sports drinks should be consumed only when physical activity is continuous for more than an hour. After exercise, children should rehydrate with 0.3 oz per pound of a child's weight for each hour of exercise. Another way to think about this is replacing the weight lost during the activity. Children should drink from bottles, rather than drinking fountains to ensure they are drinking enough. Lastly, to ensure that fluids are being fully absorbed, all active children should eat some healthy salty foods, such as pickles, salsa or pretzels.

Word Bank

estimate	['estɪmət]	n. 估计；估价；判断 v. 估计；估价；估量；判断
athlete	['æθliːt]	n. 运动员；身强体健的人
dehydrated	[ˌdiːhaɪ'dreɪtɪd]	adj. 脱水的，缺水的；干燥的
hydration	[haɪ'dreɪʃn]	n. [化学] 水合作用
eliminate	[ɪ'lɪmɪneɪt]	v. 消除；排除；淘汰
urine	['jʊərɪn]	n. 尿
metabolism	[mə'tæbəlɪzəm]	n. [生理] 新陈代谢
potentially	[pə'tenʃəli]	adv. 可能地，潜在地
appropriate	[ə'proʊpriət]	adj. 适当的；恰当的；合适的
evaporation	[ɪˌvæpə'reɪʃn]	n. 蒸发；消失；蒸发作用；蒸发量
conduction	[kən'dʌkʃn]	n. [生理] 传导
convection	[kən'vekʃn]	n. 传送；对流
enlarge	[ɪn'lɑːrdʒ]	v. 扩大，使增大，扩展；详述
dilated	[daɪ'leɪtɪd]	adj. 扩大的；膨胀的；加宽的
radiator	['reɪdieɪtər]	n. 散热器；暖气片；辐射体
dizzy	['dɪzi]	adj. 晕眩的，使人头晕的；昏乱的；心不在焉的；愚蠢的 v. 使头晕眼花；使混乱；使茫然
bout	[baʊt]	n. 回合；较量；发作；一阵
thermoregulation	['θɜːrmoʊˌregju'leɪʃn]	n. 温度调节
mental	['mentl]	adj. 精神的；脑力的 n. 精神病患者
prepubescent	[ˌpriːpjuː'besnt]	adj. 青春期前的
lemonade	[ˌlemə'neɪd]	n. 柠檬水

Unit 7
Sports Science

non-caffeinated	[nɑːnˈkæfɪneɪtɪd]	*adj.* 不含咖啡因的
non-carbonated	[nɑːn ˈkɑːrbəneɪtɪd]	*adj.* 不含碳酸的
rehydrate	[riːˈhaɪdreɪt]	*v.* 补充水分；再水化

Phrases

blood vessel	血管
be available to	可以用来；现有的
transport to	把……运送到
muscle cramp	肌痉挛，肌肉痉挛
heat exhaustion	中暑虚脱，[内科] 中暑衰竭
heat stroke	热中暑
light headed	头晕
a loss of	损失
muscle fatigue	肌肉疲劳，肌肉疲惫
rule of thumb	经验法则
drinking fountain	（设于公共场所的）自动饮水器

Task 1 Text Organization

Read the text and fill in the blanks.

Paragraphs	Main Idea	Supporting Details
Para. 1	Proper hydration	• The problem is: _____. • It is vital for _____, _____ and _____. • Water loss from _____, _____ and _____ can lead to dehydration.

Paras. 2–4	Two reasons for children to hydrate properly	• One of the primary reasons is to _____ _____. • In addition to affecting thermoregulation, ___ _____ _____ _____.
	Two ways to determine dehydration in a child	• The easiest way is _____. • Another method is _____ _____.
Para. 5	What should active children drink?	• _____ and _____ fluids are best. • After exercise, children should rehydrate with _____ for each hour of exercise. • To ensure that fluids are being fully absorbed, all active children should eat some _____ _____.

Task 2 Reading Comprehension

Exercise 1

Read the text and decide whether the following statements are true (T) or false (F).

1. _____ By some estimates, 1/2 of child athletes are dehydrated during exercise.

2. _____ One of the primary reasons for children to hydrate properly is to maintain an appropriate temperature.

3. _____ A drop in blood pressure because of dehydration can make them light in the head with the potential for injury.

4. _____ In prepubescent children, these changes are evident at a loss of only 10% percent of body weight, leading to possible loss of coordination, decreased energy and muscle fatigue.

5. _____ Children should rehydrate slowly, but steadily, within one hour of exercising, preferably with water.

Exercise 2

Read the text and answer the following questions.

1. What is proper hydration vital for?
2. What would happen when a child's body temperature increases while exercising or being in a warm environment?
3. What might a dehydrated child suffer from?
4. If an adult lost two percent of body weight from dehydration, what would it cause?
5. What are the different levels of dehydration?

Task 3 Language in Use

Exercise 1

Match the underlined words in the left column with their corresponding meanings in the right column.

1. By some <u>estimates</u>, two-thirds of child athletes are dehydrated during exercise.	A. make larger
2. Proper hydration is vital for regulating temperature, maintaining blood volume and <u>eliminating</u> waste.	B. guesses or judgements
3. When a child's body temperature increases while exercising or being in a warm environment, the blood vessels near the surface of the skin <u>enlarge</u>.	C. taking out; getting rid of
4. A dehydrated child, however, does not have enough blood available to be <u>transported</u> to the skin and the exercising muscle at the same time.	D. the act of not having someone or something
5. Dehydrated children also risk a drop in blood pressure, which can make them feel dizzy or light headed during or immediately after a bout of exercise, with the <u>potential</u> for injury.	E. related to the mind
6. Dehydration in children can have particularly strong effects on both exercise ability and performance of <u>mental</u> and physical tasks.	F. carried or transfered
7. In adults, a <u>loss</u> of two percent of body weight from dehydration can cause considerable decreases in the ability to perform these tasks.	G. something that can develop or become actual

8. However, in prepubescent children, these changes are evident at a loss of only one percent of body weight, leading to possible loss of coordination, decreased energy and <u>muscle</u> fatigue.

9. Coaches should be aware of the risk factors for injury, such as muscle weakness and poor conditioning leading to early <u>fatigue</u>.

10. To ensure that fluids are being fully <u>absorbed</u>, all active children should eat some healthy salty foods.

H. A piece of body tissue that you contract and relax in order to move a particular part of the body

I. took in through the pores of a surface

J. the decline in ability of a muscle to generate force

Exercise 2

Select one word or phrase for each blank from a list of choices given below and fill in the blank with its correct form.

appropriate	conduct	radiator	evaporate	exhaust
potential	dilated	primary	convection	blood vessel

To maintain a (an) **1.**_____ temperature is one of the **2.**_____ reasons for children to hydrate properly. Children's bodies cool mostly through "dry" **3.**_____ and **4.**_____, which is different from adults who are cooled mostly through **5.**_____ of sweat. For example, the **6.**_____ near the surface of the skin enlarge when children's body temperature increases in a warm environment. Similar to the way a **7.**_____ works in a car, the body sends warm blood to the **8.**_____ blood vessels to release heat to the surface of the skin. A dehydrated child, however, does not have enough blood available to be transported to the skin and the exercising muscle at the same time. So, children have taken a high risk of heat-related illnesses, such as muscle cramps, heat **9.**_____ or heat stroke. Dehydrated children also have the **10.**_____ for injury when they feel dizzy or light headed during or immediately after a bout of exercise if they risk a drop in blood pressure.

Exercise 3

Translate the following sentences into English.

1. 你能估算一下这个老房子值多少钱吗？(estimate)
2. 我在 800 米半决赛中被淘汰了。(eliminate)
3. 到时候，老师可以采取适当的行动。(appropriate)

4. 工作压力会带来身心两方面的健康问题。(mental)
5. 植物可以吸收灰尘。(absorb)

Training Healthy Youth Athletes
Andrea Stracciolini and Michele LaBotz

Young athletes are faced with many unique issues that place them at increased risk for injury. In particular, individuals who specialize in one sport at an early age or train at higher volumes appear to be at a markedly higher risk for serious injury. Recent studies show highly specialized young athletes are almost twice as likely to sustain a serious overuse injury as compared to participants who are not specialized. Also, young athletes participating in more hours of sports per week than age in years (for example, more than 10 hours a week for a 10-year-old) or whose ratio of organized sports to free play time was greater than 2:1 hours per week had increased odds of having a serious overuse injury.

Recovery and Sleep

The cause of overuse injuries includes repetitive sub-maximal loading of the musculoskeletal system with inadequate rest and recovery time to allow for structural adaptation. Attention to sleep patterns is critical to this recovery in young athletes. Sleep duration appears to be an independent factor associated with injury, with a recent study showing that the athletes who slept an average of less than eight hours per night were more likely to have had an injury when compared to athletes who slept for greater than eight hours. Furthermore, fatigue-related injuries in athletes are related to sleeping less than six hours the previous night.

Athlete Development

In addition to increasing injury risk, early specialization creates multiple issues in young athletes. In 2014, the United States Olympic Committee unveiled its American Development Model (ADM) as a framework for best practices in training and developing young athletes. The goals of the ADM are to provide young athletes with early positive experiences in sport, to allow individuals to realize their athletic potential and to promote long-term participation in sport and healthy levels of physical activity.

The Basic Principles of the ADM Include:

- Universal access to sport and physical activity opportunities
- Encourage multi-sport participation
- Educated coaching at all levels of sport

• Emphasis on fun, engagement of coaches and athletes and developmentally appropriate skill acquisition and training

• Development of fundamental movement skills and physical literacy

The ADM consists of five progressive stages of training and participation. Age ranges are approximate and overlapping due to variability in rates of individual motor development:

• Stage 1: Discover, Learn and Play—12 years old or younger

Focus on fun, development of basic motor skills and opportunities for deliberate play.

• Stage 2: Develop and Challenge—10–16 years old

More focus on sport-specific skill, socialization and teamwork, emphasis on progressive training, and introduce competitive opportunities.

• Stage 3: Train and Compete—13–19 years old

Emphasis on sports-skill development, progressive training and competition appropriate for skill level.

• Stage 4: Consists of two parallel tracks—15 years old and older

Track 1: Participate and Succeed: Emphasis on fun, as well as personal challenge and achievement.

Track 2: Excel for High Performance: Focus on maximizing athletic potential.

• Stage 5: Mentor and Thrive—Active for life

Lifetime involvement in sport and healthy levels of physical activity.

Word Bank

unique	[juˈniːk]	adj. 独特的，稀罕的，独一无二的 n. 独一无二的人或物
sustain	[səˈsteɪn]	v. 维持；支撑；承担；忍受
overuse	[ˌoʊvərˈjuːs]	n. 过度使用 v. 把……使用过度
odds	[ɑːdz]	n. 概率；胜算；不平等；差别
repetitive	[rɪˈpetətɪv]	adj. 重复的
maximal	[ˈmæksɪml]	adj. 最高的；最大的；最全面的
adaptation	[ˌædæpˈteɪʃn]	n. 适应；改编；改编本，改写本
multiple	[ˈmʌltɪpl]	adj. 多重的；多样的；许多的 n. 倍数
framework	[ˈfreɪmwɜːrk]	n. 框架；结构，构架
deliberate	[dɪˈlɪbərət]	adj. 故意的；深思熟虑的；从容的
socialization	[ˌsoʊʃələˈzeɪʃn]	n. 社会化
parallel	[ˈpærəlel]	adj. 平行的；类似的，相同的 n. 平行线；对比 v. 使与……平行

Unit 7 Sports Science

Phrases

specialize in	专门研究；专门经营
ratio of	……比，比例为
musculoskeletal system	肌肉骨系统，[解剖]肌肉骨骼系统
sleep duration	睡眠持续时间
associate with	与……有关系；与……相联系
compared to	与……相比
basic principles	基本原则
universal access	普及高等教育；[计]通用存取，万能辅助，普遍接入
skill acquisition	技能获取
motor development	运动发育；动作发展
involvement in	介入，参与；受累

Critical Reading and Thinking

Read the text and decide whether the following statements are true (T) or false (F).

1. _____ Young athletes are faced with many unique issues that place them at decreased risk for injury.

2. _____ Recent studies show highly specialized young athletes are almost twice as likely to sustain a serious overuse injury as compared to participants who are adults.

3. _____ Young athletes participating in less hours of sports per week than age in years had increased odds of having a serious overuse injury.

4. _____ Sleep pattern is critical to this recovery in young athletes.

5. _____ A recent study showing that the athletes who slept an average of more than eight hours per night were more likely to have had an injury when compared to athletes who slept for less than eight hours.

6. _____ Fatigue-related injuries in athletes are related to sleeping less than eight hours the previous night.

7. _____ In addition to increasing injury risk, early specialization creates fewer issues in young athletes.

8. _____ The ADM consists of five progressive stages of training and participation.

9. _____ The first stage of ADM focuses on fun, development of basic motor skills and opportunities for deliberate play.

10. _____ The third stage of ADM aged between 10–16 years old, emphases on sports-skill development, progressive training and competition appropriate for skill level.

Translation

Translate the following sentences into Chinese.

1. Young athletes are faced with many unique issues that place them at increased risk for injury.
2. In particular, individuals who specialize in one sport at an early age or train at higher volumes appear to be at a markedly higher risk for serious injury.
3. Attention to sleep patterns is critical to this recovery in young athletes.
4. Sleep duration appears to be an independent factor associated with injury, with a recent study showing that the athletes who slept an average of less than eight hours per night were more likely to have had an injury when compared to athletes who slept for greater than eight hours.
5. The goals of the ADM are to provide young athletes with early positive experiences in sport, to allow individuals to realize their athletic potential and to promote long-term participation in sport and healthy levels of physical activity.

Part Three Listening and Speaking

Task 1

Word Bank

tremendous	[trəˈmendəs]	adj. 极大的，巨大的
helmet	[ˈhelmɪt]	n. 头盔
warm-up	[ˈwɔːmʌp]	n. 预热；准备运动
stretching	[ˈstretʃɪŋ]	n. 伸展
fluid	[ˈfluːɪd]	n. 流体，液体
worsen	[ˈwɜːrsn]	v. 使恶化

Listen to an interview with Dr. Kidman, a leading expert in youth sports, and answer the following questions.

1. How many children get injured when doing sports each year?
2. What risk do sports come with?
3. What should children wear when they play sports?
4. What should children do before games?
5. Why should children report injuries right away if they get hurt in a game?

Unit 7
Sports Science

Task 2

Word Bank

cheerleading	['tʃɪrliːdɪŋ]	n. 啦啦操运动
paralysis	[pəˈræləsɪs]	n. 麻痹；瘫痪
stunt	[stʌnt]	n. 绝技，特技
upcoming	[ˈʌpkʌmɪŋ]	adj. 即将来临的
mission	[ˈmɪʃn]	n. 使命，任务
prevention	[prɪˈvenʃn]	n. 预防；阻止
Miss Teen Minnesota International		明尼苏达州青少年国际小姐

Listen to a passage about a cheerleading accident, and decide whether the following statements are true (T) or false (F).

1. _____ The cheerleading accident resulted in the paralysis of my right leg.
2. _____ We practiced a cheerleading stunt for an upcoming competition.
3. _____ I didn't feel pain when the flyer landed on my neck for the first time.
4. _____ I didn't report my pain because I was afraid of losing my spot on the team.
5. _____ I lost in the Miss Teen Minnesota International 2012 due to my injury.

Task 3

Listen to the five sentences from the recording, repeat each sentence after it is spoken, and then write it down.

1. _____.
2. _____.
3. _____.
4. _____.
5. _____.

Task 4

Discuss the following questions in your group.

1. Have you ever got injured when doing sports? How did it happen?
2. Do you know any common sports-related injuries in children?
3. What can schools do to ensure students' sports safety on campus?
4. How can we increase children's awareness of sports safety?

University Application Letters

A university application letter helps determine whether or not you will be accepted into the university of your choice. In your letter, you should state the reasons why you are interested in that university, and other important information such as your traits, qualities, ambitions, educational background, achievements, and extra curricular activities to show that you are a good fit for the school. As a formal letter, a university application letter should include all the elements of other formal letters, especially the contact information to ensure you can be reached in time when necessary.

Here is a sample letter that is meant to inspire and guide you in your application letter writing.

Sample

Letter Box 539

Physical Performance and Development Department

University of New Mexico

Email: lynetteewer@gmail.com

December 10, 2010

Dr. John Done

Chair of Department

Physical Performance and Development Department

University of New Mexico

Dear Dr. Done,

It is with great pleasure that I submit my application packet for a Master's Degree in Physical Education in the Department of Physical Performance and Development at the University of New Mexico. I am currently completing my education in the Bachelor of University Studies at UNM, with one of my emphasis in the area of Exercise Science.

I believe the Physical Performance and Development Exercise Science Master's Degree offers me the greatest opportunity to expand my education in some very meaningful areas of interest. My career interests lead me towards an avocation of exercise science, cardiac rehabilitation and fitness prescription. I want to be very involved in improving the quality of lives of those individuals I have the opportunity to help. I also feel the faculty at the University of New Mexico is most qualified to help me attain my goals.

I see UNM as a wonderful next step for me in attaining my ambitions. I thank you for the opportunity to submit this application for your consideration. Please contact me if there is anything else I need to provide. I am looking forward to communicating with you in the near future.

Sincerely,
Lynette Ewer
Lynette Ewer

Follow-up Writing

You are a fourth-year student at the Department of Exercise and Health Science, Nanjing Sport Institute. And you would like to join the UNM physical therapy program for the 2013—2014 academic year. Write an application letter to Kathy Dieruf, the Admissions Chairperson of UNM School of Medicine. His office is in HSSB Room 204.

Unit 8

Skating

Part One Knowledge Preparation

Skating involves any sport or recreational activity which consists of traveling on surfaces or on ice using skates. There are several different kinds of skating depending on the nature of the surface: ice skating (moving on ice by using ice skates), roller skating (traveling on surface with roller skates) and snow skating (using a hybrid of skateboard and a snowboard on snow). For ice skating, figure skating and speed skating are the two sub-events frequently seen in the Olympic Games and they have different rules in games.

Olympic figure skating consists of four events or disciplines: ladies' singles, men's singles, pairs and ice dancing. In men's and ladies' singles, skaters display a high level of aesthetic form and technical skill under a great amount of pressure. Each competition comprises two parts—a short program, worth 33.3% of the final score, and a free skate, worth 66.7%. Pairs skating is performed in unison by partners who execute daring and difficult overhead lifts, throw jumps and spins. The key to pairs skating is the exact timing and simultaneous movement. The pairs discipline, like singles, has a short program, worth 33.3% of the final score with eight required elements and a longer free skate, worth 66.7%.

滑冰是指所有以运动或休闲为目的，使用冰鞋或冰刀在冰面或是硬质地面上的运动。根据运动平面的差异，可以分为滑冰（使用冰刀鞋在冰质表面的运动）、轮滑（使用轮滑鞋在硬质地面的运动）和滑雪（使用滑板在雪面上的运动）。在奥运赛场上比较常见的有两种滑冰项目——花样滑冰和速滑，其规则各不相同。

奥运会花样滑冰设有4个奖项或分项，分别是：女子单人滑、男子单人滑、双人滑和冰上芭蕾。男女单人滑比赛要求运动员在承受很大压力的同时，展示高超的美感与技艺。比赛包括两个部分——占总分33.3%的短节目和占总分66.7%的自由滑。双人滑要求两名运动员协调一致地完成高难度的大胆托举、抛跳和旋转。双人滑的关键是把握好节拍的准确及动作的一致性。双人滑项目与单人滑一样，也由一个占总分33.3%的、有8组规定动作的短节目和一个稍长、占总分66.7%的自由滑组成。

Unit 8 Skating

Part Two Reading

Speed Skating

1 Skating began as a rapid form of transportation across frozen lakes and rivers. The Dutch were arguably the earliest pioneers of skating. They began using canals to maintain communication by skating from village to village as far back as the 13th century. Skating eventually spread across the channel to England, and soon the first clubs and artificial rinks began to form.

2 The first known skating competition is thought to have been held in the Netherlands in 1676. However, the first official speed skating events were not held until 1863 in Oslo, Norway. In 1889, the Netherlands hosted the first World Championships, bringing together Dutch, Russian, American and English teams. The International Skating Union (ISU) was founded in 1892 in Scheveningen in the Netherlands, and has governed the sport of speed skating ever since. Speed skating appeared for the first time in 1924 at the first Winter Olympic Games in Chamonix. Initially, only men were allowed to participate. It was only at the Lake Placid Games in 1932 that women were authorized to compete in speed skating, which was then only a demonstration sport. It was not until the 1960 Games in Squaw Valley that women's speed skating was officially included in the Olympic program.

3 Short track (of indoor) speed skating was first practiced in Europe at the end of the 19th century and quickly spread to the United States and Canada, where it became extremely popular. The events almost always follow the European system, until the Olympic Games at Lake Placid in 1932, the Americans organized American-style events, i.e. with a mass start and "pack" style of racing. This decision brought about a boycott by many European competitors, which allowed the Americans to win the four gold medals. This system would give birth to short track speed skating, which was added to the Olympic program in Albertville in 1992.

4 Short track involves a pack start or a group competition. Here four to six skaters race to be the first person across the finishing line. This type of race has a mass start, where all the skaters start from the starting line at the same time. Another type of short track skating is a relay race. A relay team of four members must compete in tandem, such that each skater of a team takes at least one round of the track. Standard distances include 500 meters (4.5 laps), 1,000 meters (9 laps) and 1,500 meters (13.5 laps).

5. A race is divided into heats, quarterfinals, semifinals and finals. Competitors advance to the next round by the process of elimination, where the top two skaters in a round are declared the victors. The skating track is oval shaped and is 111.12 m long, enclosed within a standard 60 m × 30 m ice rink. If a skater skates on the inside of the track, the distance becomes shorter and he/she has an advantage. That is why the starting positions of the skaters are decided by lots. The track must be skated in a counterclockwise manner. The official starter will fire a pistol into the air to start the race. The skaters are allowed only one false start; if more than one, they are disqualified. The skater in the lead has right of way and can pass other skaters but must avoid collisions. The inside skater is responsible for collisions, if any occur, unless clearly obstructed by his or her opponent.

Word Bank

pioneer	[ˌpaɪəˈnɪr]	n. 先锋；拓荒者 v. 开辟；倡导，提倡
canal	[kəˈnæl]	n. 运河；[地理] 水道
artificial	[ˌɑːrtɪˈfɪʃl]	adj. 人造的；仿造的
host	[hoʊst]	v. 主持；当主人招待 n. [计] 主机；主人；主持人
govern	[ˈgʌvərn]	v. 管理；支配；统治；控制
authorize	[ˈɔːθəraɪz]	v. 批准，认可；授权给；委托
demonstration	[ˌdemənˈstreɪʃn]	n. 示范；证明；示威游行
boycott	[ˈbɔɪkɑːt]	v. 联合抵制；拒绝参加 n. 联合抵制
relay	[ˈriːleɪ]	n. 接力
tandem	[ˈtændəm]	n. 串联；一前一后
elimination	[ɪˌlɪmɪˈneɪʃn]	n. 消除；淘汰；除去
counterclockwise	[ˌkaʊntərˈklɑːkwaɪz]	adj. 反时针方向的 adv. 反时针方向
pistol	[ˈpɪstl]	n. 手枪；信号枪
disqualify	[dɪsˈkwɑːlɪfaɪ]	v. 取消……的资格
collision	[kəˈlɪʒn]	n. 碰撞，冲突；（意见，看法的）抵触
obstruct	[əbˈstrʌkt]	v. 妨碍；阻塞；遮断

Proper Names

Dutch	荷兰（的）；荷兰人（的）；荷兰语（的）
Netherlands	荷兰
Oslo	奥斯陆（挪威城市名）
Norway	挪威
Scheveningen	席凡宁根海滩（荷兰著名海滨度假胜地）
Chamonix	霞慕尼
Lake Placid	普莱西德湖（美国纽约州内陆湖）

Squaw Valley 斯阔谷（美国加州）
Albertville 艾伯特维尔

Task 1 Text Organization

Read the text and fill in the blanks.

Paragraphs	Key Words	Supporting Details
Paras. 1–2	Introduction of speed skating	• Skating began as a rapid form of _____ across frozen lakes and rivers. • The _____ were arguably the earliest pioneers of skating. • The first known skating competition is thought to have been held in the _____ in 1676. However, the first official speed skating events were not held until _____ in Oslo, Norway. • In 1889, _____ hosted the first World Championships. • _____ has governed the sport of speed skating since 1892. • It was not until the _____ Games in _____ that women's speed skating was officially included in the Olympic program.
Para. 3	Introduction of short track speed skating	• It was first practiced in _____. • The Americans organized American-style events, i.e. with a mass start and "pack" style of racing in 1932 Games. • This brought about a boycott by many European competitors, which allowed the Americans to win the four gold medals.
Paras. 4–5	Types and rules of short track speed skating	• types: (1) _____, all the skaters start from the starting line at the same time; (2) _____, members must compete in tandem. • rules: (1) A race is divided into_____ _____; (2) The skating track is _____ shaped and is _____ long, enclosed within a standard _____ ice rink;

119

Paras. 4–5	Types and rules of short track speed skating	(3) The skater skating _____ of the track has an advantage; (4) The track must be skated in a _____ manner; (5) The skaters are allowed only one false start, otherwise they are _____; (6) The skater in the lead has right of way and can pass other skaters but must avoid _____.

Task 2 Reading Comprehension

Exercise 1

Read the text and decide whether the following statements are true (T) or false (F).

1. _____ The Dutch were arguably the earliest pioneers of skating.
2. _____ The first official speed skating events have been held in the Netherlands in 1676.
3. _____ Speed skating appeared for the first time in 1924 at the first Olympic Winter Games in Chamonix and only men were allowed to participate.
4. _____ Short track speed skating involves a pack start and a relay race.
5. _____ The skater skating on the outside of the track has an advantage because of the short distance.

Exercise 2

Read the text and answer the following questions.

1. What is the purpose of skating originally?
2. When were the first official speed skating events held?
3. At which Winter Olympic Games did short speed skating become a full-medal sport?
4. What are the three standard distances in relay race in the short track speed skating?
5. In what situation were the skaters disqualified?

Task 3 Language in use

Exercise 1

Match the underlined words in the left column with their corresponding meanings in the right column.

1. The Dutch were arguably the earliest <u>pioneers</u> of skating.   A. the race competition finished by the athletes one after another

Unit 8
Skating

2. Skating eventually spread across the channel to England, and soon the first clubs and <u>artificial</u> rinks began to form.

3. The International Skating Union (ISU) was founded in 1892 in Scheveningen in the Netherlands, and has <u>governed</u> the sport of speed skating ever since.

4. Initially, only men were allowed to <u>participate</u>.

5. It was only at the Lake Placid Games in 1932 that women were <u>authorized</u> to compete in speed skating, which was then only a demonstration sport.

6. This decision brought about a <u>boycott</u> by many European competitors, which allowed the Americans to win the four gold medals.

7. Another type of short track skating is a <u>relay</u> race.

8. Competitors advance to the next round by the process of <u>elimination</u>.

9. The skaters are allowed one false start; if more than one, they are <u>disqualified</u>.

10. The skater in the lead has right of way and can pass other skaters but must avoid <u>collisions</u>.

B. bumps or dashes

C. the first people to do something

D. protest

E. man-made; made by hands

F. controled; organized

G. not having the right to complete the competition

H. take part in; join in

I. knockout match

J. gave right to (by government)

Exercise 2

Select one word for each blank from a list of choices given below and fill in the blank with its correct form.

host	appear	communication	official	transport
short	spread	add	rapid	boycott

Skating is a well-known **1.**_____ form of **2.**_____ across frozen lakes and rivers which began in Dutch. As far back as the 13th century, canals had been used to maintain **3.**_____ by skating from village to village. The first known skating competition is thought to have been held in the Netherlands in 1676, and the first **4.**_____ speed skating events were not held until 1863 in Oslo, Norway. It was in the year of 1889 that the Netherlands **5.**_____ the first World Championships, bringing together

Dutch, Russian, American and English teams. And it was the first time in 1924 that speed skating **6.**_____ at the first Olympic Winter Games in Chamonix.

7._____ track speed skating was not appeared until at the end of the 19th century and was first practiced in Europe. Then it was quickly **8.**_____ to the United States and Canada. In the Olympic Games at Lake Placid in 1932, the Americans organized American-style events, which brought about a **9.**_____ by many European competitors. The system of short track speed skating was **10.**_____ to the Olympic program in Albertville in 1992.

Exercise 3

Translate the following sentences into English.
1. 2008 年，北京成功举办了夏季奥运会。(host)
2. 因为这种产品需要前期调研，所以直到 2015 年才投入市场。(authorize)
3. 由于这一方案引起了广泛的争议，我们需要重新考虑。(bring about)
4. 约翰在速滑刚开始时，跟对手发生了碰撞，所以被取消了比赛资格。(collision; disqualify)
5. 大雨阻碍了我们的行程。(obstruct)

Text B

Ice Skating: Steps to Success

Karin Kunzle-Watson, one of the world's most prominent ice skating instructors—nine-time Swiss National Champion, former Professional World Champion, and one of skating's best instructors—began her amateur and professional skating career at the age of six. A former champion at the novice and junior levels, Karin earned seven Swiss national senior titles during her career. She has also placed in many international competitions, including seven European championships, five world championships, and one Olympic appearance. She is one of the few people in the world to have passed Gold Tests (qualifying tests for competition at the highest levels) in all areas of skating—singles, pairs, and dance. Karin is also an accomplished instructor, having been School Director and Head Professional at the Skating School of St. Gervais and Megeve (France) and School Director of the Skating School of San Mateo (U.S.). She presently travels internationally to attend her students' competitions, to teach, and to conduct skating and coaching seminars. Her students consistently rank highly in national and international competitions.

Stephen J. DeArmond, MD, PhD, began ice skating at the age of 47 because he wanted a high-energy, low-impact exercise that was enjoyable enough to do several times weekly. Karin Kunzle-Watson's approach to basics helped him to become an accomplished recreational skater.

Stephen helped Karin organize her lessons into five basic principles—the foundation of the book *Ice Skating: Steps to Success*—and directed the illustration and photography. Stephen is a Professor of Neuropathology and Neurology at the University of California, San Francisco, with special research interests in the effects of aging on the central nervous system and skeletal muscle. In the book, Stephen shares insights on the health benefits of ice skating, especially to improve both strength and coordination, as well as information on the causes and prevention of injuries.

With the help of Karin Kunzle-Watson and Stephen J. DeArmond, thousands of people who never skated before can now find their way in this beautiful, though technically difficult, sport. Read it and try it, have fun, get your body physically involved and your mind mentally working!

Word Bank

instructor	[ɪnˈstrʌktər]	*n.* 指导书；教员，指导者
amateur	[ˈæmətər]	*adj.* 业余的；外行的 *n.* 业余爱好者；外行
novice	[ˈnɑːvɪs]	*n.* 初学者，新手
accomplished	[əˈkɑːmplɪʃt]	*adj.* 有造诣的；完成的；熟练的，有技巧的
recreational	[ˌrekriˈeɪʃənl]	*adj.* 娱乐的，消遣的；休养的
illustration	[ˌɪləˈstreɪʃn]	*n.* 说明；插图；例证，图解
neuropathology	[ˌnjʊroʊpəˈθɒlədʒɪ]	*n.* 神经病理学
neurology	[nʊˈrɑːlədʒi]	*n.* 神经病学；神经学
skeletal	[ˈskelətl]	*adj.* 骨骼的；像骨骼的；骸骨的

Critical Reading and Thinking

Read the text and decide whether the following statements are true (T) or false (F).

1. _____ Karin began her career as an ice skater very early in her childhood.
2. _____ Karin earned seven Swiss national senior gold medals during her career.
3. _____ Karin is the only one of the few people in the world to have passed Gold Tests.
4. _____ Karin presently travels internationally to attend her students' competitions, to teach, and to conduct skating and coaching seminars.
5. _____ Stephen began ice skating at the age of 47 because he wanted a high-energy, low-impact exercise because he likes it very much.
6. _____ Karin helps Stephen to write his book.
7. _____ Stephen is a teacher at the University of California.
8. _____ Stephen is interested in Neuropathology and Neurology and has some achievements on the effects of aging on the central nervous system and skeletal muscle.

9. _____ Stephen is the writer of the book *Ice Skating: Steps to Success*.
10. _____ Many people have the interest in ice skating, with the help of the book *Ice Skating: Steps to Success*.

Translation

Translate the following sentences into Chinese.

1. A former champion at the novice and junior levels, Karin earned seven Swiss national senior titles during her career.
2. She presently travels internationally to attend her students' competitions, to teach, and to conduct skating and coaching seminars.
3. Her students consistently rank highly in national and international competitions.
4. Stephen J. DeArmond, MD, PhD, began ice skating at the age of 47 because he wanted a high-energy, low-impact exercise that was enjoyable enough to do several times weekly.
5. With the help of Karin Kunzle-Watson and Stephen J. DeArmond, thousands of people who never skated before can now find their way in this beautiful, though technically difficult, sport.

Part Three Listening and Speaking

Task 1

Word Bank

misfortune [ˌmɪsˈfɔːrtʃuːn] *n.* 不幸；灾祸

Listen to an interview with a speed skater shortly after a race and answer the following questions.

1. What happened to Jessica in the race?
2. Was she injured in the race?
3. What did she need to do in each race?
4. What did she say about the Olympics?
5. What is exciting for Jessica?

Unit 8
Skating

Task 2

Word Bank

backbone	['bækboʊn]	n. 支柱；主干
debut	[deɪ'bjuː]	n. 初次登台；开张
controversial	[ˌkɑːntrə'vɜːrʃl]	adj. 有争议的，有争论的
expel	[ɪk'spel]	v. 驱逐；开除
scuffle	['skʌfl]	n. 混战；扭打
rink	[rɪŋk]	n. 溜冰场
Sochi		索契（俄罗斯城市）
Vancouver		温哥华（加拿大港市）
Salt Lake City		盐湖城（美国城市）

Listen to a news report about China's short-track speed skating team and choose the best answer to each question.

1. What competition are many athletes making preparations for?
   A. The Salt Lake City Games.   **B.** The Vancouver Games.
   C. The Sochi Games.   **D.** The Pyeongchang Games.

2. Who won the first gold medal for China at the Winter Olympics?
   A. Yang Yang.   **B.** Wang Meng.
   C. Zhou Yang.   **D.** Liang Wenhao.

3. How many gold medals did China win at the Winter Olympic Games in Vancouver?
   A. 1.   **B.** 2.
   C. 3.   **D.** 4.

4. Why was Wang Meng expelled from the national team in 2011?
   A. Because she had a scuffle with a teammate.
   B. Because she had a scuffle with the coach.
   C. Because she had a scuffle with the team leader.
   D. Because she had a scuffle with a referee.

Task 3

Listen to the five sentences from the recording, repeat each sentence after it is spoken, and then write it down.

1. _____.
2. _____.
3. _____.
4. _____.
5. _____.

Task 4

Discuss the following questions in your group.

1. Who is your favorite speed skater? Why?
2. Do you know the rules of speed skating? Give a brief introduction.
3. What equipment does a skater need in speed skating?
4. What do you know about China's short-track speed skating team?

Job Application Letters

A job application letter is often attached to, or accompanying a résumé to introduce you as a job seeker to potential employers and explaining your suitability for the desired position. A job application letter is usually constructed of three parts: the introduction, body, and conclusion. The purpose of the introduction is to specify why you are writing and to say a few things about yourself, such as your college and your major. The introduction also gives you the opportunity to praise to the company for some specific quality it possesses. The body of your letter should draw connections from your past experiences and education to the specific skills required for the job you are seeking. The conclusion must bring the letter to a cordial but brief close. While asking for a follow-up interview in the conclusion, you must sound confident, yet never pushy.

In Part Four of Unit 1, you can find a sample job application letter requesting a position as a table tennis trainer.

Unit 8 Skating

Follow-up Writing

You have learned from the campus online bulletin board that XYZ Corporation is in need of skating instructors to develop their business. Write an application letter to the company to state your willingness to have the job, present your experiences in skating instruction and express your expectation for an interview. You can use the following information to begin your letter.

27 University Avenue
Brooklyn NY 11288
April 11, 2003

Ms. Mary Jones
Director of Campus Relations
XYZ Corporation
54 West Third Street
Albany, NY 10056

Dear Ms. Jones,

_____

_____

_____

_____

Glossary

absorb	[əb'zɔːrb]	v. 吸收；吸引；承受	U3TA
accompany	[ə'kʌmpəni]	v. 陪伴，伴随；伴奏	U1TB
accomplished	[ə'kaːmplɪʃt]	adj. 有造诣的；完成的；熟练的，有技巧的	U8TB
accomplishment	[ə'kaːmplɪʃmənt]	n. 成就；完成；技艺，技能	U6TB
acrobat	['ækrəbæt]	n. 杂技演员，特技演员	U5TA
adaptation	[ˌædæp'teɪʃn]	n. 适应；改编；改编本，改写本	U7TB
additional	[ə'dɪʃənl]	adj. 附加的，额外的	U3TA
adopt	[ə'daːpt]	v. 采取；接受；收养；正式通过	U2TB
aerobic	[e'roʊbɪk]	adj. 需氧的；有氧健身的	U3TA
affix	[ə'fɪks]	v. 贴上；署名	U5TA
agenda	[ə'dʒendə]	n. 议程；日常工作事项；日程表	U1TA
aggressor	[ə'gresər]	n. 侵略者，侵略国；挑衅者	U1TB
all-out	[ˌɔːl'aʊt]	adj. 全部的；竭尽全力的；毫无保留的	U2TB
amateur	['æmətər]	adj. 业余的；外行的	
		n. 业余爱好者；外行	U8TB
amend	[ə'mend]	v. 修改；改善，改进	U2TA
amidst	[ə'mɪd]	prep. 在……当中	U6TA
animate	['ænɪmeɪt]	v. 使有生气；使活泼	U5TA
ankle	['æŋkl]	n. 踝关节，踝	U3TA
anticipate	[æn'tɪsɪpeɪt]	v. 预期，期望；占先，抢先；提前使用	U2TB
antics	['æntɪks]	n. 滑稽动作，古怪姿态	U5TA
apparel	[ə'pærəl]	n. 服装；衣服	U6TB
application	[ˌæplɪ'keɪʃn]	n. 申请；应用	U1TA
apply	[ə'plaɪ]	v. 申请；适用	U3TB
appointee	[əˌpɔɪn'tiː]	n. 被任命者	U1TA
appropriate	[ə'proʊpriət]	adj. 适当的；恰当的，合适的	U7TA
approximately	[ə'praːksɪmətli]	adv. 大约，近似地，近于	U1TB

aptitude	['æptɪtuːd]	n. 天资，天赋	U1TB
aquatic	[ə'kwætɪk]	adj. 水生的；水栖的；在水中或水面进行的 n. 水上运动；水生植物或动物	U6TB
arise	[ə'raɪz]	v. 出现；上升；起立	U2TB
artificial	[ˌɑːrtɪ'fɪʃl]	adj. 人造的；仿造的	U8TA
assist	[ə'sɪst]	v. 帮助；促进	U3TA
athlete	['æθliːt]	n. 运动员；身强体健的人	U7TA
auspicious	[ɔː'spɪʃəs]	adj. 吉兆的，吉利的；幸运的	U5TA
authorize	['ɔːθəraɪz]	v. 批准，认可；授权给；委托	U8TA
backhand	['bækhænd]	n. 反手拍；反手抽击	U2TB
bamboo	[ˌbæm'buː]	n. 竹，竹子	U5TA
ban	[bæn]	v. 禁止	U1TA
beloved	[bɪ'lʌvd]	adj. 心爱的；挚爱的	U6TB
beverage	['bevərɪdʒ]	n. 饮料	U3TB
bleacher	['bliːtʃər]	n.（运动场的）露天看台，露天座位	U6TA
blessing	['blesɪŋ]	n. 祝福；赐福；祷告	U5TA
blister	['blɪstər]	n. 水疱	U3TA
bond	[bɑːnd]	n. 密切联系	U6TB
boost	[buːst]	v. 提高，增加；鼓励；举起；为……做宣传	U4TB
boredom	['bɔːrdəm]	n. 厌倦；令人厌烦的事物	U6TB
bout	[baʊt]	n. 回合；较量；发作；一阵	U7TA
boycott	['bɔɪkɑːt]	v. 联合抵制；拒绝参加 n. 联合抵制	U8TA
campaign	[kæm'peɪn]	v. 参加竞选；从事运动	U4TB
canal	[kə'næl]	n. 运河；[地理] 水道	U8TA
cardiovascular	[ˌkɑːrdioʊ'væskjələr]	adj. [解剖] 心血管的	U3TA
casual	['kæʒuəl]	adj. 随便的；非正式的	U1TB
certificate	[sər'tɪfɪkət]	n. 证明书；文凭，结业证书	U4TA
chant	[tʃænt]	n. 圣歌，赞美诗；吟唱	U6TA
chip	[tʃɪp]	n. 筹码	U4TA
circulatory	['sɜːrkjələtɔːri]	adj. 循环的	U3TA
collision	[kə'lɪʒn]	n. 碰撞；冲突；（意见，看法的）抵触	U8TA
colon	['koʊlən]	n. [解剖] 结肠	U3TA

comb	[koʊm]	n. 梳子	U1TB
commission	[kəˈmɪʃn]	n. 委员会；佣金	U1TA
competitor	[kəmˈpetɪtər]	n. 竞争者；对手	U4TA
concentration	[ˌkaːnsnˈtreɪʃn]	n. 集中；专心	U3TA
conditioning	[kənˈdɪʃənɪŋ]	n. 调节；条件；训练，健身训练	U3TA
conduct	[kənˈdʌkt]	v. 组织并实施	U2TA
conduction	[kənˈdʌkʃn]	n. [生理] 传导	U7TA
confirm	[kənˈfɜːrm]	v. 证实；批准；确定	U4TB
confrontation	[ˌkaːnfrənˈteɪʃn]	n. 对抗，对峙；面对；遭遇	U4TA
consecutive	[kənˈsekjətɪv]	adj. 连贯的，连续不断的	U2TA
conservation	[ˌkaːnsərˈveɪʃn]	n. 保存；保持；保护	U2TB
consistency	[kənˈsɪstənsi]	n. 坚持；一致性	U3TB
constantly	[ˈkaːnstəntli]	adv. 不断地；时常地	U3TB
constitution	[ˌkaːnstəˈtuːʃn]	n. 章程；宪法；体制	U1TA
containment	[kənˈteɪnmənt]	n. 牵制（遏制）政策	U1TB
continent	[ˈkaːntɪnənt]	n. 大陆；洲；陆地	U2TA
continental	[ˌkaːntɪˈnentl]	adj. 大陆的；大洲的	U1TA
convection	[kənˈvekʃn]	n. 传送；对流	U7TA
coordination	[koʊˌɔːrdɪˈneɪʃn]	n. 协调，调和	U5TA
counterclockwise	[ˌkaʊntərˈklaːkwaɪz]	adj. 反时针方向的 adv. 反时针方向	U8TA
counting	[kaʊntɪŋ]	n. 计算	U4TA
cub	[kʌb]	n. 幼兽	U5TB
curve	[kɜːrv]	v. 使弯曲；使成曲线	U4TA
custodian	[kʌˈstoʊdiən]	n. 管理人；监护人；保管人	U6TA
customarily	[ˌkʌstəˈmerəli]	adv. 通常，习惯上	U3TA
deceive	[dɪˈsiːv]	v. 欺骗，行骗	U2TB
deception	[dɪˈsepʃn]	n. 欺骗，欺诈；骗术	U2TB
decisively	[dɪˈsaɪsɪvli]	adv. 果断地，决然地	U2TB
deduce	[dɪˈduːs]	v. 演绎；推论，推断；追溯根源	U4TA
defect	[ˈdiːfekt]	n. 缺点；缺陷	U4TB
dehydrated	[ˌdiːhaɪˈdreɪtɪd]	adj. 脱水的，缺水的；干燥的	U7TA
delegation	[ˌdelɪˈgeɪʃn]	n. 代表团	U1TB

deliberate	[dɪˈlɪbərət]	adj. 故意的；深思熟虑的；从容的	U7TB
delicate	[ˈdelɪkət]	adj. 微妙的；精美的，雅致的；柔和的；易碎的；纤弱的	U2TB
demonstration	[ˌdemənˈstreɪʃn]	n. 示范；证明；示威游行	U8TA
depict	[dɪˈpɪkt]	v. 描述；描画	U5TA
despite	[dɪˈspaɪt]	prep. 尽管，不管	U3TB
determine	[dɪˈtɜːrmɪn]	v. 决定；判定，判决；限定	U2TA
dilated	[daɪˈleɪtɪd]	adj. 扩大的；膨胀的；加宽的	U7TA
diplomacy	[dɪˈploʊməsi]	n. 外交，外交手腕	U1TA
diplomatic	[ˌdɪpləˈmætɪk]	adj. 外交的，外交上的；老练的	U1TB
disputable	[dɪˈspjuːtəbl]	adj. 可争议的	U6TA
disputed	[dɪˈspjuːtɪd]	adj. 有争议的	U1TA
disqualify	[dɪsˈkwɑːlɪfaɪ]	v. 取消……的资格	U8TA
dizzy	[ˈdɪzi]	adj. 晕眩的，使人头晕的；昏乱的；心不在焉的；愚蠢的 v. 使头晕眼花；使混乱；使茫然	U7TA
docile	[ˈdɑːsl]	adj. 温顺的，驯服的	U5TB
don	[dɑːn]	v. 穿上（衣服）	U6TA
double	[ˈdʌbl]	n.（常用复数）双打	U2TB
downwards	[ˈdaʊnwərdz]	adv. 向下，往下	U2TB
dropshot	[ˈdrɑːpʃɑːt]	n. 近网短球	U2TB
efficient	[ɪˈfɪʃnt]	adj. 有效率的；有能力的；生效的	U3TA
eligibility	[ˌelɪdʒəˈbɪləti]	n. 适任；合格；选举或参赛资格	U1TA
eliminate	[ɪˈlɪmɪneɪt]	v. 消除；排除；淘汰	U7TA
elimination	[ɪˌlɪmɪˈneɪʃn]	n. 消除；淘汰；除去	U8TA
embargo	[ɪmˈbɑːrgoʊ]	n. 贸易禁令，禁运	U1TB
emblem	[ˈembləm]	n. 标志；徽章，纹章	U1TB
encounter	[ɪnˈkaʊntər]	n. 遭遇；偶然碰见	U1TB
endurance	[ɪnˈdʊrəns]	n. 忍耐力；忍耐；持久	U3TA
enforce	[ɪnˈfɔːrs]	v. 实施，执行	U1TB
enlarge	[ɪnˈlɑːrdʒ]	v. 扩大，使增大，扩展；详述	U7TB
ensure	[ɪnˈʃʊr]	v. 保证，确保；使安全	U2TA
entertainment	[ˌentərˈteɪnmənt]	n. 娱乐，消遣；款待	U5TB

essential	[ɪˈsenʃl]	adj. 基本的；必要的；本质的	U6TA
establish	[ɪˈstæblɪʃ]	v. 建立，创办；安置	U2TA
estimate	[ˈestɪmət]	n. 估计；估价；判断	
		v. 估计；估价；估量；判断	U7TA
evaporation	[ɪˌvæpəˈreɪʃn]	n. 蒸发；消失；蒸发作用；蒸发量	U7TA
eventually	[ɪˈventʃuəli]	adv. 最后，终于	U1TB
evolution	[ˌiːvəˈluːʃn]	n. 进化；发展；演变	U4TB
exchange	[ɪksˈtʃeɪndʒ]	n. 交换；交流；交易所；兑换	U1TB
exhausting	[ɪɡˈzɔːstɪŋ]	adj. 使筋疲力尽的；使耗尽的	U2TB
expedition	[ˌekspəˈdɪʃn]	n. 远航；考察队，远征军	U4TA
exploit	[ɪkˈsplɔɪt]	v. 利用；开发；剥削；开采	U2TB
exponentially	[ˌekspəˈnenʃəli]	adv. 迅速增长地，迅猛发展地	U6TA
facet	[ˈfæsɪt]	n. 小平面；方面	U4TB
fervent	[ˈfɜːrvənt]	adj. 强烈的；炽热的；热心的	U6TA
finalize	[ˈfaɪnəlaɪz]	v. 最后定下，使（计划、交易等）确定	U1TA
finisher	[ˈfɪnɪʃər]	n. 整理工；修整器；决定性的事件；最后优胜者	U2TA
firsthand	[ˌfɜːrstˈhænd]	adv.（来源、资料等）第一手地，直接地	U6TB
flamboyant	[flæmˈbɔɪənt]	adj. 炫耀的；艳丽的；火焰似的	U1TB
flexible	[ˈfleksəbl]	adj. 灵活的；柔韧的；易弯曲的	U2TB
flick	[flɪk]	n. 弹开；快速地轻打；轻打声	U2TB
forecourt	[ˈfɔːrkɔːrt]	n. 前院；前场	U2TB
forehand	[ˈfɔːrhænd]	n. 正手击球；正手；正拍	U2TB
format	[ˈfɔːrmæt]	n. 格式；版式；赛制	U2TA
formation	[fɔːrˈmeɪʃn]	n. 形成；构造；编队	U2TB
foul	[faʊl]	v. [体] 违反规则	U4TA
found	[faʊnd]	v. 创立，建立，创办	U1TA
framework	[ˈfreɪmwɜːrk]	n. 框架；结构，构架	U7TB
freeze	[friːz]	v. 冻结，冷冻；僵硬	U6TA
frenemy	[ˈfrenəmi]	n. 亦敌亦友	U6TA
frequency	[ˈfriːkwənsi]	n. 频率；频繁	U3TA
fringe	[frɪndʒ]	n. 边缘	U5TA
gear	[ɡɪr]	n.（用于特定活动的）设备；服装	U6TA

word	pronunciation	meaning	unit
gleam	[gliːm]	n. 微光；闪光；瞬息的一现	U6TA
glue	[gluː]	n. 胶，胶水	U1TA
glue	[gluː]	v. 黏合	U5TA
goodwill	[ˌɡʊdˈwɪl]	n. 好意，亲善，友善	U1TB
govern	[ˈɡʌvərn]	v. 管理；支配；统治；控制	U8TA
hand-in-hand	[ˈhændinˈhænd]	adj. 并进的；手拉手的；亲密的	U6TB
heed	[hiːd]	v. 注意，留心	U3TB
heel	[hiːl]	n. 脚后跟，踵	U3TA
hesitantly	[ˈhezɪtəntli]	adv. 迟疑地，踌躇地	U1TB
host	[hoʊst]	v. 主持；当主人招待 n. [计] 主机；主人；主持人	U8TA
household	[ˈhaʊshoʊld]	n. 家庭；同住一所房子的人	U6TA
humbly	[ˈhʌmbli]	adv. 谦逊地	U6TB
hurricane	[ˈhɜːrəkən]	n. 飓风，暴风	U5TA
hydration	[haɪˈdreɪʃn]	n. [化学] 水合作用	U7TA
ideal	[aɪˈdiːəl]	adj. 理想的；完美的	U2TB
identical	[aɪˈdentɪkl]	adj. 同一的，完全相同的	U2TB
illustration	[ˌɪləˈstreɪʃn]	n. 说明；插图；例证，图解	U8TB
inclined	[ɪnˈklaɪnd]	adj. 趋向于……的	U6TB
inclusive	[ɪnˈkluːsɪv]	adj. 包容的	U1TA
incorporate	[ɪnˈkɔːrpəreɪt]	v. 包含；结合	U1TB
indispensable	[ˌɪndɪˈspensəbl]	adj. 不可缺少的，绝对必要的；责无旁贷的	U3TA
individual	[ˌɪndɪˈvɪdʒuəl]	adj. 个人的；个别的；独特的	U3TA
inspire	[ɪnˈspaɪər]	v. 激发；鼓舞；启示，使生灵感	U2TA
institute	[ˈɪnstɪtuːt]	v. 开始（调查）；制定；创立	U1TA
instructor	[ɪnˈstrʌktər]	n. 指导书；教员，指导者	U8TB
intentional	[ɪnˈtenʃnl]	adj. 故意的，蓄意的；策划的	U3TA
intercept	[ˌɪntərˈsept]	v. 拦截，截断；窃听	U2TB
interpreter	[ɪnˈtɜːrprɪtər]	n. 解释者；口译者，翻译	U1TB
inter-zone	[ɪntəˈzoʊn]	adj. 地区间的；地带间的	U2TA
isolated	[ˈaɪsəleɪtɪd]	adj. 孤立的，隔离的	U1TB
itch	[ɪtʃ]	n. 痒	U5TB
jersey	[ˈdʒɜːrzi]	n. 运动衫，毛线衫	U6TA

khaki	[ˈkɑːki]	n. 卡其裤；卡其服装	U6TA
laborious	[ləˈbɔːriəs]	adj. 勤劳的；艰苦的；费劲的	U6TA
launch	[lɔːntʃ]	v. 发起，发动	U5TB
legacy	[ˈlegəsi]	n. 遗赠；遗产	U1TB
leisurely	[ˈliːʒərli]	adj. 悠闲的，从容的	U3TA
lemonade	[ˌleməˈneɪd]	n. 柠檬水	U7TA
lid	[lɪd]	n. 盖子；眼睑	U2TA
lifespan	[ˈlaɪfspæn]	n. 寿命	U3TA
lottery	[ˈlɑːtəri]	n. 彩票；碰运气的事	U6TA
manoeuvring	[məˈnuːvərɪŋ]	n. 部署；调遣；谋略	U2TB
market	[ˈmɑːrkɪt]	v. 在市场上出售；做买卖	U6TB
mascot	[ˈmæskɑːt]	n. 吉祥物；福神（亦作 mascotte）	U5TB
mask	[mæsk]	n. 面具	U5TB
massage	[məˈsɑːʒ]	n. 按摩；揉	U3TB
mature	[məˈtʃʊr]	adj. 成熟的；仔细考虑过的	U4TA
maximal	[ˈmæksɪml]	adj. 最高的；最大的；最全面的	U7TB
mental	[ˈmentl]	adj. 精神的；脑力的 n. 精神病患者	U7TA
merchandise	[ˈmɜːrtʃəndaɪs]	n. 商品；货物	U6TB
metabolism	[məˈtæbəlɪzəm]	n. [生理] 新陈代谢	U7TA
mileage	[ˈmaɪlɪdʒ]	n. 英里数	U3TB
milestone	[ˈmaɪlstoʊn]	n. 里程碑	U3TB
momentum	[moʊˈmentəm]	n. 势头；[物] 动量；动力；冲力	U2TB
motivate	[ˈmoʊtɪveɪt]	v. 使有动机，激发……的积极性	U3TB
mountaineering	[ˌmaʊntnˈɪrɪŋ]	n. 登山运动，爬山	U4TB
multiple	[ˈmʌltɪpl]	adj. 多重的；多样的；许多的 n. 倍数	U7TB
mystical	[ˈmɪstɪkl]	adj. 神秘的；神秘主义的	U3TA
national	[ˈnæʃnəl]	n. 国民	U1TB
netshot	[ˈnetʃɑːt]	n. 网前放小球，网前球	U2TB
neurology	[nʊˈrɑːlədʒi]	n. 神经病学；神经学	U8TB
neuropathology	[ˌnjʊroʊpəˈθɑːlədʒi]	n. 神经病理学	U8TB
non-caffeinated	[nɑːnˈkæfɪneɪtɪd]	adj. 不含咖啡因的	U7TA
non-carbonated	[nɑːn ˈkɑːrbəneɪtɪd]	adj. 不含碳酸的	U7TA

单词	音标	释义	位置
norm	[nɔːrm]	n. 标准，规范	U6TA
novice	[ˈnɑːvɪs]	n. 初学者，新手	U8TB
numerous	[ˈnuːmərəs]	adj. 许多的，很多的	U1TA
nutrition	[nuˈtrɪʃn]	n. 营养；营养学；营养品	U3TB
obesity	[oʊˈbiːsəti]	n. 肥大，肥胖	U3TA
obstruct	[əbˈstrʌkt]	v. 妨碍；阻塞；遮断	U8TA
odds	[ɑːdz]	n. 概率；胜算；不平等；差别	U7TB
officially	[əˈfɪʃəli]	adv. 正式地；官方地	U2TA
opening	[ˈoʊpnɪŋ]	n. 开始；机会；通路；空缺的职位	U1TA
opponent	[əˈpoʊnənt]	n. 对手，反对者，敌手	U2TB
opposing	[əˈpoʊzɪŋ]	adj. 反对的；相对的；对面的	U2TA
optimal	[ˈɑːptɪməl]	adj. 最佳的，最理想的	U3TA
original	[əˈrɪdʒənl]	adj. 原始的，最初的；独创的，新颖的	U1TB
originate	[əˈrɪdʒɪneɪt]	v. 发源；发生	U3TA
overcompensate	[ˌoʊvərˈkɑːmpenseɪt]	v. 过度补偿	U3TB
overuse	[ˌoʊvərˈjuːs]	n. 过度使用 v. 把……使用过度	U7TB
oxygen	[ˈɑːksɪdʒən]	n. [化学] 氧气	U3TA
pad	[pæd]	n. 衬垫；护具	U3TA
panel	[ˈpænl]	n. 咨询或研讨小组	U1TA
parallel	[ˈpærəlel]	adj. 平行的；类似的，相同的 n. 平行线；对比 v. 使与……平行	U7TB
participant	[pɑːrˈtɪsɪpənt]	n. 参与者	U2TA
participation	[pɑːrˌtɪsɪˈpeɪʃn]	n. 参与	U1TB
passionate	[ˈpæʃənət]	adj. 热情的；热烈的，激昂的	U6TA
pedicure	[ˈpedɪkjʊr]	n. 修趾甲术；足部护理	U3TB
phase	[feɪz]	n. 时期	U2TA
physician	[fɪˈzɪʃn]	n. [医] 医师，内科医师	U3TA
pioneer	[ˌpaɪəˈnɪr]	n. 先锋；拓荒者 v. 开辟；倡导，提倡	U8TA
pistol	[ˈpɪstl]	n. 手枪；信号枪	U8TA
platform	[ˈplætfɔːrm]	n. 平台	U6TB

plinth	[plɪnθ]	n. 柱基，底座	U2TA
pool	[puːl]	n. 小组；撞球；水塘；共同资金	U2TA
portion	[ˈpɔːrʃn]	n. 部分	U3TB
portray	[pɔːrˈtreɪ]	v. 描绘；扮演	U5TB
postpone	[poʊˈspoʊn]	v. 使……延期	U3TB
potentially	[pəˈtenʃəli]	adv. 可能地，潜在地	U7TA
prepubescent	[ˌpriːpjuːˈbesnt]	adj. 青春期前的	U7TA
present	[prɪˈzent]	v. 提出；介绍；呈现；赠送	U2TA
prestigious	[preˈstɪdʒəs]	adj. 有名望的，享有声望的	U2TA
previous	[ˈpriːviəs]	adj. 以前的，早先的	U1TA
principle	[ˈprɪnsəpl]	n. 原则；法则	U3TB
prominent	[ˈprɑːmɪnənt]	adj. 突出的，显著的；杰出的，卓越的	U2TB
prop	[prɑːp]	n. 道具；支柱，支撑物	U5TA
prostate	[ˈprɑːsteɪt]	n. [解剖] 前列腺	U3TA
qualify	[ˈkwɑːlɪfaɪ]	v. 取得资格，有资格	U2TA
radiator	[ˈreɪdieɪtər]	n. 散热器；暖气片；辐射体	U7TA
rally	[ˈræli]	n.（网球、乒乓球等）连续对打；集会 v. 团结；集合	U1TA
rearcourt	[ˈrɪəkɔːrt]	n. 后场；后院	U2TB
recap	[ˈriːkæp]	n. 扼要重述	U6TA
recreational	[ˌrekriˈeɪʃənl]	adj. 娱乐的，消遣的；休养的	U8TB
reference	[ˈrefrəns]	v. 引用	U1TB
rehydrate	[riːˈhaɪdreɪt]	v. 补充水分；再水化	U7TA
reign	[reɪn]	n. 君主的统治；君主统治时期	U4TA
relay	[ˈriːleɪ]	n. 接力	U8TA
repetitive	[rɪˈpetətɪv]	adj. 重复的	U7TB
resistance	[rɪˈzɪstəns]	n. 阻力；抵抗，反抗；抵抗力	U1TA
resonate	[ˈrezəneɪt]	v. 共鸣；共振	U6TB
respective	[rɪˈspektɪv]	adj. 分别的，各自的	U2TA
revamp	[ˈriːvæmp]	v. 修改；修补；翻新	U2TA
reverse	[rɪˈvɜːrs]	v. 颠倒，倒转	U2TB
rhythmically	[ˈrɪðmɪkli]	adv. 有节奏地	U5TA
ridiculously	[rɪˈdɪkjələsli]	adv. 可笑地，荒谬地	U6TA

round-robin	[ˌraʊndˈrɑːbɪn]	n. 循环赛；[计] 循环	U2TA
royal	[ˈrɔɪəl]	adj. 皇家的	U5TB
schedule	[ˈskedʒuːl]	n. 时间表；计划表	U3TB
scratch	[skrætʃ]	v. 抓，搔	U5TB
seek	[siːk]	v. 寻求；寻找	U1TA
segment	[ˈsegmənt]	n. 段；部分	U5TA
semifinalist	[ˌsemiˈfaɪnəlɪst]	n. 成功晋级半决赛的选手，半决赛选手	U2TA
server	[ˈsɜːrvər]	n. 发球员	U1TA
service	[ˈsɜːrvɪs]	n. 发球	U1TA
session	[ˈseʃn]	n. 会议；会期；开庭期；学期；一段时间	U4TB
shed	[ʃed]	v. 摆脱	U3TB
shuttlecock	[ˈʃʌtlkɑːk]	n. 羽毛球；毽子	U2TB
similarity	[ˌsɪməˈlærəti]	n. 类似；相像性，相仿性	U4TA
single	[ˈsɪŋgl]	n.（常用复数）单打比赛；（美）独身者；单程票	U2TB
skeletal	[ˈskelətl]	adj. 骨骼的；像骨骼的；骸骨的	U8TB
skip	[skɪp]	v. 跳过；遗漏	U3TB
slicing	[slaɪsɪŋ]	n. 切断，切片；限制	U2TB
slightly	[ˈslaɪtli]	adv. 些微地，轻微地；纤细地	U3TA
slogan	[ˈsloʊgən]	n. 口号；标语	U1TB
smash	[smæʃ]	n.& v. 扣球；破碎；冲突	U2TB
snack	[snæk]	n. 小吃，快餐；零食	U3TB
sneaker	[ˈsniːkər]	n. 运动鞋	U3TB
socialization	[ˌsoʊʃələˈzeɪʃn]	n. 社会化	U7TB
spectacular	[spekˈtækjələr]	adj. 壮观的，惊人的	U6TA
spectator	[ˈspekteɪtər]	n. 观众；旁观者	U1TA
sponsorship	[ˈspɑːnsərʃɪp]	n. 赞助；倡议；保证人地位	U4TB
stability	[stəˈbɪləti]	n. 稳定性；坚定，恒心	U3TA
stake	[steɪk]	n. 桩，棍子	U5TB
stamina	[ˈstæmɪnə]	n. 毅力；精力；活力	U5TB
startlingly	[ˈstɑːrtlɪŋli]	adv. 惊人地，使人惊奇地	U6TA
steady	[ˈstedi]	adj. 稳定的；不变的；沉着的	U3TA
stealth	[stelθ]	n. 秘密；隐蔽	U3TB

strengthen	['streŋθn]	v. 加强，巩固	U6TB
stroke	[stroʊk]	n.（打、击等的）一下；（游泳或划船的）划；中风	U2TB
subscription	[səb'skrɪpʃn]	n.（电视或频道）付费	U6TB
subsequent	['sʌbsɪkwənt]	adj. 后来的，随后的	U2TB
subsequently	['sʌbsɪkwəntli]	adv. 随后，其后；后来	U5TB
substantially	[səb'stænʃəli]	adv. 实质上；大体上；充分地	U2TB
subtle	['sʌtl]	adj. 微妙的；精细的；敏感的	U2TB
suffering	['sʌfərɪŋ]	n. 受难；苦楚	U3TB
summit	['sʌmɪt]	n. 顶峰；高层会议；最高阶层	U4TA
sustain	[sə'steɪn]	v. 维持；支撑；承担；忍受	U7TB
swallow	['swaːloʊ]	v. 完全相信；忍受；吞下	U6TA
swing	[swɪŋ]	v. 使旋转；挥舞；悬挂	U5TA
synchronize	['sɪŋkrənaɪz]	v. 使……合拍；使……同步	U5TA
systematic	[ˌsɪstə'mætɪk]	adj. 系统的，体系的，有系统的	U2TB
tandem	['tændəm]	n. 串联；一前一后	U8TA
target	['tɑːrgɪt]	v. 把……作为目标；规定……的指标	U6TB
tease	[tiːz]	v. 戏弄，挑逗；取笑	U5TA
teeming	['tiːmɪŋ]	adj. 多产的，丰富的；热闹的	U6TA
terrace	['terəs]	n. 平台；梯田；阳台	U5TB
terrain	[tə'reɪn]	n. 地形，地势；地面，地带	U4TA
territory	['terətɔːri]	n. 领土；领域；范围	U1TA
thaw	[θɔː]	n. 解冻；融雪	U1TB
thermoregulation	['θɜːrməʊˌregjuˈleɪʃn]	n. 温度调节	U7TA
tournament	['tʊrnəmənt]	n. 锦标赛，联赛；比赛	U2TA
transitional	[træn'zɪʃənl]	adj. 过渡的	U1TA
treadmill	['tredmɪl]	n. 跑步机	U3TA
trigger	['trɪgər]	v. 引发，引起，触发	U1TB
trim	[trɪm]	v. 削减；修剪；整理；装点	U2TA
triumph	['traɪʌmf]	n. 胜利，凯旋；欢欣	U6TA
troupe	[truːp]	n. 剧团	U5TB
trump	[trʌmp]	v. 胜过；打出王牌赢	U2TA
tumble	['tʌmbl]	v. 摔倒；滚动；打滚	U5TB

tumbling	['tʌmblɪŋ]	adj. 翻滚的；歪斜状的	U2TB
typically	['tɪpɪkli]	adv. 代表性地；作为特色地；通常	U2TB
umpire	['ʌmpaɪər]	n. 裁判员；仲裁人	U4TA
unanimously	[ju'nænɪməsli]	adv. 全体一致地，无异议地	U4TB
union	['juːniən]	n. 联盟；协会	U1TA
unique	[ju'niːk]	adj. 独特的，稀罕的，独一无二的 n. 独一无二的人或物	U7TB
universal	[juːnɪ'vɜːrsl]	adj. 普遍的，通用的；宇宙的，全世界的	U1TA
urine	['jʊərɪn]	n. 尿	U7TA
venerable	['venərəbl]	adj. 庄严的；值得尊敬的；珍贵的	U2TA
via	['vaɪə]	prep. 通过；经由	U2TA
viable	['vaɪəbl]	adj. 可行的	U1TA
victorious	[vɪk'tɔːriəs]	adj. 胜利的，凯旋的	U2TA
vigorous	['vɪɡərəs]	adj. 有力的；精力充沛的	U3TB
vision	['vɪʒn]	n. 视力，视觉；美景	U4TA
vulnerable	['vʌlnərəbl]	adj. 易受攻击的；易受伤害的；有弱点的	U2TB
waltz	[wɔːls]	v. 跳华尔兹舞；旋转；轻快地走	U6TA
warrior	['wɔːriər]	n. 战士，勇士	U5TB
wave	[weɪv]	v. 挥手示意；使成波浪形	U1TB
writhe	[raɪð]	v. 翻滚；蠕动	U5TB